Alexander Rogers

In Persia's golden Days

Alexander Rogers

In Persia's golden Days

ISBN/EAN: 9783743316461

Manufactured in Europe, USA, Canada, Australia, Japa

Cover: Foto ©ninafisch / pixelio.de

Manufactured and distributed by brebook publishing software (www.brebook.com)

Alexander Rogers

In Persia's golden Days

BY

ROBERT J. GRIFFITHS, M.A., LL.D.,

AND

ALEXANDER ROGERS.

LONDON:

GRIFFITHS AND SON,
ST. PAUL'S BUILDINGS, E.C.
1889.

TO

His Imperial Majesty,

NASIR-UL-DEEN SHAHINSHAH,

WE,

THE JOINT AUTHORS OF THE FOLLOWING SKETCH OF THE
CAREER OF ONE OF YOUR MAJESTY'S PREDECESSORS
ON THE ILLUSTRIOUS THRONE OF PERSIA,
BEG TO BE ALLOWED TO DEDICATE THE
WORK TO YOU IN TOKEN OF
WELCOME ON YOUR ARRIVAL
ON ENGLAND'S
SHORES.

R. J. GRIFFITHS.
A. ROGERS.

Accepted on behalf, and by command, of the Shahinshah.

MALCOM KHAN,
Ambassador.

IN PERSIA'S GOLDEN DAYS.

CHAPTER I.

THE PRINCE'S CRIME.

IT was a bright, dry, radiant morning full of the promise of a scorching afternoon. In the city of Madáin, one of Persia's many capitals, when the House of Sassân ruled over the great empire of Irân, people had but little leisure on this morning of mornings to think much about the weather. The busy hum of the bazaar was hushed for once. The main street, where the palaces of the late king, Khusroo I., of his son, the reigning king, Hormuz, of Bahram Choobeen, the great captain of Persia's hosts, and of many another great noble—that street was deserted and empty, for King Hormuz was in his diván, or hall of justice, sitting in judgment upon no ordinary prisoner. Look well at the defendant as he passes into the hall of justice, for he is the king's son. In years to come his generals will expel the Romans from Asia and Africa. The bounds of his empire will be equalled only by those of Darius the Great. He will live a conqueror, and he will die—ah, well! we shall see how he died. This morning Khusroo, the second of his name, passes into the diván with a frown on his young handsome face. It is a brave, strong face, marked though it is with traces which show that he is not free from some of the vices of Eastern princes. Into the hall he passes. Let us go with him.

In the centre was a daïs raised three steps above the floor. Over it was spread a carpet of the richest Oriental brocade. In the middle of the daïs was a cushion large enough to form a very cosy seat. It was stuffed to the depth of several inches with fine soft sheep's wool, and at the back was another cushion upon which the king could lean. Over it all was spread a rich cloth of gold, embroidered with green leaves and crimson flowers. The steps of the daïs were covered with silver tissue, which threw out into strange relief the pure white of the walls in the background. Glance for a moment at those walls, for they are worth looking at. They are made of the finest lime, of shells brought for the purpose from the far-off shores of the Persian Gulf. See how these shells have been worked into a thousand quaint geometrical forms, intermingled with small mirrors of stained glass of myriad hues exquisitely blended together. Pause at the door before the trial commences, and look out from the courtyard at the city beyond. The diván, like the cities of refuge, is approached by four broad, straight roads. On either side of each of them is a channel of masonry wherein flows the water that nurtures the orange trees, upon which everywhere the eye rests gratefully. Beyond the trees you may catch glimpses of beds of the red rose of Persia. The still, hot air is heavy with the fragrance of the flowers, drowsy with the sweetness of a thousand orange groves, and the boundless wealth of flowers beyond. Of a truth, King Hormuz knows where and how to live.

It is time, however, to turn round and re-enter the hall; the great nobles of the State have now arrived. For them cushions similar to those on the daïs have been placed round the hall, but with this difference, that they are unadorned save for a bunch of natural roses placed upon each of them. In the courtyard and in the hall itself the crowd is dense, the spectators craning their necks and holding their hands to their ears in the hope of catching some strange utterance from within. Yes, it was a silent crowd, and there was good reason for its silence, for behind the royal judge stood a grim, gaunt figure, immovable apparently as a statue. It was the Ethiopian executioner, armed with a bright scimitar. At the royal nod the proudest head in all that great assembly would have rolled in the dust. Interest in the trial, tempered, perhaps, by the presence of that terrible figure, kept the crowd dumb, although it was by no means deaf.

King Hormuz sat on the daïs. For some reason

best known to themselves he was unpopular with his subjects; but, nevertheless, he was every inch a king, although there was but little in his dress to betoken his rank. Around his waist, indeed, was a richly jewelled belt, and the one glittering diamond aigrette in his tall, black, triangular hat of the finest Astracan wool flashed back the rays of light as the king's head moved. Otherwise he was plainly dressed in white; but the khanjar, or dagger, in his belt—a weapon without which no Persian of rank in those days ever appeared in public—was so richly jewelled that the fine gold of its handle was hardly visible. By his side lay the royal sword of State. Behind him was not only the executioner, but also attendants with fly-whisks to protect the royal person from these nuisances. On either side of him was a chobdar, or macebearer, with the insignia of his office on his shoulder—a short, slightly carved club, covered with beaten gold, embossed with flowers.

On the side cushions, attired in white, sat, as we have said, the great officers of State. First of all, on the right was the Vazir, or prime minister; immediately below him was the royal treasurer, distinguished by a bunch of keys instead of a dagger at his waist; on the left were the chief Mobed, or high-priest, the royal astrologer, the royal scribe, and half a score of other great dignitaries of Persia; last of all, was the culprit, the youth of twenty summers, who was to be tried. With folded arms he stood on the steps leading to the daïs, and a close observer could have detected in that swarthy countenance, half Jewish, half Persian, a suppressed inclination to laugh. If he had laughed, it would not have been wonderful.

For after all this prototype of our own fifth Henry had done nothing amazingly wrong. The facts were that Prince Khusroo, tired with a day's hunting, had gone into a village, where he took too much wine, and forthwith proceeded to make a night of it with his companions. He began by turning a villager out of his house, and taking possession of it. One of his slaves next proceeded to get food without payment from another villager; and, last of all, into this same villager's field the prince's horse was turned, much to the detriment of the wheat crop standing in it.

The king's judgment, upon learning the facts, was that all the prince's hunting apparatus should be given to the man whose house had been taken possession of, that the slave should become the property of the man whom he had forced to feed him, and that the horse that had eaten the crop should be punished by having its feet cut off. The people shouted that the judgment of the king was as that of Solomon, on whom be peace! The royal scribe was proceeding to register the decree according to the law of the Medes and Persians, which altereth not, when the prince called to him:

"Stay thy hand, O Mirza! Let not the bright page of justice be stained with the blot of error; and let not the sun-like splendour of the light of equity be overshadowed by the dark cloud of unbecoming punishment!"

Then turning to the king, he continued:

"Sun of the country! The Almighty's shade! Than Phœnix' wings more blest thy royal aid! Hath thy slave permission to endeavour to pierce the pearl of the royal ear with the needle of persuasion?"

The king having extended to him his right hand in token of approval, Khusroo continued:

"O king, may thy good fortune last for ever! Thy slave has committed a fault, and so has thy slave's slave. Let us both, who have sown the seed of evil, reap the harvest of punishment, as the lord of justice hath decreed. On our head and eyes may it be! But this dumb beast of no understanding hath but trodden the path in which he was placed. He hath but eaten that which was given him; nor could he know whether the food was lawful or unlawful."

"An eye for an eye, and a tooth for a tooth," answered the king. "His feet have gone upon a wrong road, and should be prevented from doing so again!"

"True, O king," replied the prince; "but hath the diver of thy mind brought up from the deep sea of thine intellect the pearl of reflection? Hast thou considered that in cutting off the feet of the horse thou dost also tear up the root of its sweet life?"

"Nay," said the king, "that would be going beyond the law. What says our spiritual adviser?" And he turned towards the chief Mobed.

That functionary immediately rose, and prostrating himself before the king, said:

"The words of the refuge of the world are as a

fountain of wisdom, and as the water of life to the thirsty soul!"

"Rise, my trusty adviser!" Then said the king: "Write, Mirza, the royal decree. The horse shall live; but he to whom it belongs shall pay ten times the value of the crop destroyed. Thus would we protect our subjects even against the oppression of princes. And thou, my son, approach!"

Thus saying, the king undid from Khusroo's waist the golden chain which was the token that one of the royal house was on his trial in the king's court of justice, and said: "And thou, my son, beware for the future, lest the demon of intoxication lead thy foot astray into the wilderness of evil."

It will thus be seen that the situation of Prince Khusroo before the king was not at all unlike that of Henry V. of England when, as Prince of Wales, he made the acquaintance of his father's Chief Justice. In the present instance the king seemed not at all indisposed to let matters pass much more easily for the culprit, when suddenly Prince Khusroo knelt at his father's feet, and presenting the sword that lay by the side of the cushion, exclaimed:

"Punishment I can bear, but not that of the king's displeasure. I humble my neck in the dust before thee! Cut off my wretched head; but forget afterwards the crime of which I have been guilty, and let my memory remain in the royal favour!"

At this point many of the impressionable people in the outer court burst into loud lamentations of "Hai!

hai! Shall the black crow of darkness, which the gold-scattering sun of fortune was driving to its dismal nest, again obscure with its ill-omened wing the morning star of Ajam? Shall the white page of the king's rule be reddened by the foul stain of his innocent son's blood? Hai! hai! O king, restrain thy hand!"

Gently then the royal father raised his kneeling son, and, kissing him on the forehead, said:

"Go in peace: thou art my son again."

As Khusroo, after profound prostrations, arose and backed out of the royal presence, the people shouted: "May the king's life be prolonged, and his fortune last for ever! Sorrow to him who doth not wish thee joy! Ruin to him who desireth not thy prosperity! May the king live for ever!"

Then King Hormuz rose, and went into the diván-i-khás, where in private audience he transacted with his ministers the business of the State, and his judgment was likened throughout the land to that of Solomon for its wisdom.

CHAPTER II.

THE LADY BEYOND THE WESTERN HILLS.

SHUBDEEZ was the prince's horse, and Khusroo's first act when the trial was over was to visit the stable of his steed; as with most other Eastern soldiers, his horse was an object of intense interest to him. As he paced up and down in Shubdeez's stable, this is how he apostrophized that famous animal: "Thanks be to God that I have saved thee! Oh, darling of my soul! how could I have borne life without thee! The wild ass of the desert would have rejoiced, and the fleet buck of the Salt Plain would have leapt for joy, hadst thou been slain; but where would Khusroo's heart have been? It would quickly have gone to corruption in the earth of thy honoured grave. No more mounted on my lightning-paced steed should I have hunted the nimble gazelle, or, spear in hand, charged home upon the lithe panther, well knowing that thou wouldst bear me safely beyond the reach of his spring."

Then, as he caressed Shubdeez, he continued:

"Dost thou remember the day when, sore wounded and bleeding in the midst of foes, and almost despairing of life, I threw myself upon thy neck, and thou, lashing out with thy heels, didst bear me along the road of escape to my camp? Come, Shubdeez, come, and thou shalt have thy favourite lick of salt from thy master's hand."

He loosed the rope at Shubdeez's head, and, followed closely by the horse, he went to his own apartments. There Shubdeez had the promised lick of salt, and, having been handed over to an attendant, was taken back to its picket, where, like all desert-bred horses, it remained without tent or shelter; the prince himself passed into an inner court. In the centre was, of course, a fountain. It was surrounded by beds of narcissus and tulips—favourite flowers both of them in Persia—and adjoining them was a luxurious couch shaded from the rays of the afternoon sun as it began to sink into the golden west. For a time reclining on the couch he remained absorbed in thought. Then he gave three strokes with the fingers of one hand on the palm of the other. This was a signal to a slave who brought him his kalioon, or water-pipe, an Eastern luxury as precious in Persia as a good cigar is here. Let me describe it. The bowl was of the finest porcelain of a turquoise blue. It would have delighted the eyes of modern *bric-à-brac* collectors could they have laid hands on that priceless pipe. The tube through which the smoke was to be inhaled was about a yard in length, so that the vapour, even if it had not been passed through the purest rose-water, would have been perfectly cool before it reached the mouth. The mouthpiece, of what in India would have been called a hookah, was a special gift of his father, given to him on his last birthday. It was of the finest amber, and was studded with costly pearls. Khusroo had just commenced smoking when one of the nobles of the court, an intimate friend of his, came in. After respectfully kneeling down and touching the ground with his forehead, he sat down in the half-kneeling posture to be seen in old Persian pictures, with his feet drawn under the long skirt of his white coat.

"If the king of my world will give command," Shápur said, "thy slave will pour into the royal ear the words of truth."

"First of all, friend," said Khusroo, "let me order wine, that thy throat be not parched with the hot wind of talk."

To this proposition his friend demurred. He gave Khusroo some excellent advice as to some of his recent escapades in this direction, but he accepted an offer of sherbet and a kalioon. These were brought by a slave. For some time the two smoked in silence, broken only by the drip of the fountain and the bubbling of the water in the kalioon bottles.

After a time Khusroo spoke. He reminded Shápur that the latter had just returned from a tour behind the Western Hills, and asked him if he had found nothing new or strange there.

"Surely, my prince," said Shápur, "thy slave has seen many things, the like of which the winner of fancy has never painted upon the tablets of thought;

but strangest of all has it seemed to me that a tribe of women should have a woman for their ruler, whom they obey of their own will, and should conduct the affairs of the State without the assistance of a man, and should, in short, live precisely as if there were no men in existence."

"That is a very funny story," said the prince, musingly; "but where do these remarkable people exist?"

"Their ruler, O prince," Shápur replied, "is one Maheen Bánoo, who men say is in purity like the fresh fallen snow on Damávend's head, in wisdom and judgment the equal of Jumsheed, and in loving qualities such that her women care not to look upon the face of a man. The heir is her brother's daughter, who has been thus described to thy slave. Her eyes are black as the water of life, her two lips like rubies of the purest water, her eyebrows like the bent bow, her locks like the spikenard, her stature like that of the cypress, her gait graceful as the partridge's, her nose like a silver sword that has cut an apple in two. The writer of time would fail were he to endeavour to tell all her charms on the page of eternity, and the chronicles of the age would not contain all her virtues. Like the moon traversing the heavens in her grace, so is she among her seventy constellations of fair maidens, each fairer than a Peri, and more sweet-tongued than nightingales of Paradise."

"What is the fair one's name?" eagerly inquired Khusroo.

"Her name," replied Shápur, "suits her as doth thy name, Purweez, the Victorious, describe my prince's perfections. It is Sheereen, the 'Sweet,' that gratifies all mouths and attracts all hearts."

"Thou spreadst a net of enchantment before the bird of my desire," Khusroo continued. "But, alas! the cruel cloud of distance obscures the moon of *my* hope. Is the treasury of thy invention empty that thou canst not provide me with the coin of stratagem by which I may behold her beauty and refresh my soul with her sweetness?"

"Maheen Bánoo, my prince," observed Shápur, "is not only a great ruler, but a powerful magician as well. She has a mirror which reflects from far and wide the image of any stranger who approaches her camp, and long ere the steed of his wish can advance upon the plain of meeting the eye of her discernment will pierce the cloak of his concealment, and lay bare the secret of his coming."

"But," suggested the prince, "the lamb does not always remain by its mother's side: it sometimes may be led away by sweeter pasture to fields distant from its ordinary feeding-place; so Sheereen cannot be always with Maheen Bánoo. Might not the panther of our stratagem lay secret wait for this lamb of our intent when it had thus strayed from its fold, and carry it off to the den of our longing?"

"A wise man will not reckon too much on the feebleness of his foe," Shápur remarked. "The panther might find that the lamb was guarded by the dogs of the shepherd, and Sheereen's seventy maidens, without whom she does not go abroad, would be more than a match for many men, though each of these were a Purweez."

"Friend Shápur," the prince interrupted, impatiently, "thou dost but bind the pigeon more firmly in the fowler's snare. Flutter as it will, my heart cannot escape, and Sheereen I must possess. Unlock, therefore, the door of thy wisdom and bring forth the weapons of thy contrivance, so that we may be rewarded with the booty of our endeavours."

"Be it upon the head and eyes of thy slave, O prince!" cheerfully answered his trusty henchman. "The Jinn of opposition must have the wit of Solomon and the valour of Roostum that shall keep the Peri of thy desire from thy embrace. But now, to set to work. I must at once to Khuzistán, where is to be found this ruby of great price. Give me Shubdeez, thy well-loved steed, that I may on my errand speed, and trust that with my mother-wit I may full soon accomplish it."

"Shubdeez shalt thou have," was Khusroo's reply. "And when I whisper in his ear that he goes on his master's errand, neither hunger nor thirst shall discourage his fiery soul, neither storm nor torrent shall stay his impetuous course, till thou return again with good tidings of how thou hast sped. In how long may I hope to see thee once more?"

"Even on Shubdeez," Shápur said, "the journey must be one of three or four days, and with the return must take up seven or eight. Then how long I shall be there will depend on my friend's good fortune. By-the-bye, had we not better consult the royal astrologer as to the most auspicious hour for starting?"

"Certainly," was the prince's answer; "leave that to me, and go and prepare thyself for thy journey. What escort wilt thou have?"

"What thou wouldst do secretly with thy left hand," said his friend, "let not thy right hand know. I will ride alone, and in the disguise of a groom, so that if the eyes of the prying should recognize Shubdeez on the way, I may have wherewith to answer their inquisitive inquiries in saying I go by thy command to seek for him a worthy mate among the noble breed of the Western Hills."

"Go, then," said Khusroo. "Khoodá háfiz! God be thy protector!"

"Khoodá háfiz!" he answered. "To-morrow's dawn, at latest, should see me on my way."

CHAPTER III.

THE CAMP OF THE AMAZONS.

THE royal astrologer conveniently discovered that next morning at daybreak would be the most auspicious time for the commencement of Shápur's journey. Shubdeez displayed his usual powers of speed and endurance, and on the evening of the third day carried his rider to a hermitage at the foot of a hill in the neighbourhood of which the nomads' camp was known to be. They were now in their summer quarters on the plain at the western foot of the hills that divide Ajam from Khuzistán. The hermit, a magnificent old man with a flowing white beard, who had left behind him the cares and sorrows of the world to contemplate in solitude the beneficence of the deity, gave Shápur such hospitable entertainment as he could afford, in the shape of parched grain to eat and pure spring-water to drink, with a shake-down of dry grass for himself and the horse, and directed him in the morning to where he had been told the day-camp of Sheereen and her seventy maidens was to be. When not engaged in the chase, they usually chose for their retreat during the day some secluded valley among the hills, where, sheltered by trees from the heat of the sun, and provided with water from some mountain stream, they could while away the time, not exactly "in maiden meditation, fancy free," but in preparing their arms for hunting, in looking after the accoutrements of their horses, and in such other amusements and trifling as might come into the heads of a bevy of young and lively girls who had not the resources of Mudie's or the Grosvenor Gallery at their command. On the present occasion their bivouac—for their tents were left behind in the camp at headquarters, to which they all retired as darkness approached—was in a cosy nook, from which, surrounded as it was by high rocks covered with the light graceful foliage of the bamboo, there was apparently no exit but by the pathway up the bed of a stream by which it was entered. The stream itself trickled down from the rock at the opposite end, forming tiny casades, which, with the brown fern-clothed rock at their sides, contrasted prettily with the varied tints of the bamboo thickets that surrounded them, and with the darker shades of the tamarind and other lofty trees that grow wherever they could find space on the banks and the open places in the valley. About half-way up the valley the little river fell over a rock about ten feet in height into a basin of pellucid water of some depth, large enough to form a natural bath, the pebbles and water-plants at the bottom of which were all distinctly visible. Unruffled by any breeze, the water showed the reflection of every rock and bush near it, so that each point and leaf and spray stood out in relief in Nature's mirror in a manner inimitable by the clumsy hand of mortal artist. Horses were picketed in groups of twos and threes beneath the grateful shade of the tall tamarinds, and scattered about among them and in clusters throughout the valley Sheereen's attendants were employed in various ways. Some with arms bared up to the elbow rubbed the sleek coats of their favourite steeds till they shone again, using neither curry-comb nor brush; some led, or rather were followed by, their animals to water at the stream, for every horse came at its mistress's call; some polished the points of their arrows and glittering spear-heads, or prepared new strings for their bows; others attended to the cooking of their simple meal of unleavened cakes toasted over charcoal fires, and a few wove garlands of the wild flowers with which the valley was carpeted to wreath round the head of their mistress, who reclined on a mossy bank in the midst of a merry group, some of whom threw water in sport over others who splashed and frolicked in the pool beneath the cascade; whilst ever and anon was heard the sound of a lute accompanying a sweet voice that sang some legend of the deeds of their warlike ancestors, or improvised a soul-stirring description of adventure in the chase.

As Shápur cautiously approached this scene of enchantment—he had left Shubdeez behind him at the hermit's cave—concealing himself behind rocks and bushes as he came, these words, sung to a lively air, caught his ear:

"Off with the falcon ere dawning of day !
Ride ere the deer from the plain speeds away !
In its restraining leash hold back the hound,
Lest tow'rds the mountain the nimble buck bound !
 Ride, sisters, ride,
 On your swift steeds of pride,
 Keen as the eagle that hovers the plain.
 Glistening spear in hand,
 Start forth, a merry band,
 Heading the deer ere their shelter they gain ! "

The song was evidently a favourite one, for the chorus was caught up by fifty voices, and echoed again and again through the valley. Then the single voice began once more :

"Ere the bright dove of day with its pinion of light
Shall drive back to darkness the black crow of night,
And the violet's scent on the breeze of the morn
Through day's opening gate to our senses is borne,
 Wake, sisters wake !
 Your soft couches forsake !
 Sluggard is she who waits for the sun,
 Lion and wolf and bear
 Day to their dens will scare,
 Hiding in caves ere her course has begun.

Hushed is the sound of the nightingale's trill—
Soon will the sun's arrows strike on the hill,—
Yet swifter than these must the huntresses be
On steeds like the wind, and their hearts just as free.
 Ride, sisters, ride,—
 On your fleet steeds of pride
 Swoop like the falcon that thirsts for his prey ;
 Nor tighten the rein
 Till the chase is in vain,
 And the antelope hides in the thicket away ! "

And the valley resounded again as the girls from different sides sang alternate lines of the chorus, and danced, and as it were flung them at each other across the stream.

Then Sheereen said to the singer: "Dilárám, my heart's repose, thou art a poetess as well as a huntress, and we never tire of hearing thy songs; but we must not always harp upon one string, as if we were never weary of killing. Sing us a song of a gentler strain.

Dilárám replied: "It was after our last day's hunt on the banks of the 'Zindah Rood' that, as it grew dusk in the evening, I wandered out of the camp to enjoy the sea-breeze that had just begun to blow up from the Gulf. Seeing by the light of the waning moon some dark object behind a bush, I walked towards it, and before I was perceived had time to make out that it was a doe in vain endeavouring to give suck to a fawn which, from having an arrow that had pierced it still sticking in its leg, was unable to move to reach the nurture offered, and lay panting and faint with hunger. Painfully the mother bleated and tried to get the little one to rise. She had no doubt watched it from afar with a mother's eye, but not dared to come nearer till darkness was coming on. As I went on, she naturally bounded away; and as I knew the fawn would soon be set upon by jackals and prowling beasts of prey, I picked it up and carried it home. That night I lay awake, after I had taken the arrow out and bound up the wound, and poured milk down the little one's throat, and composed an air and words, which I will sing if my princess desires."

"Sing, sing!" at once cried a chorus of voices. "The nightingale hides his head under his wing from envy of thee, sweet Diláràm!"

And Diláràm struck a plaintive minor chord, and commenced her song:

> "The sun had long set and the evening was still;
> The sough of the night wind was heard on the hill.
> Awoke from their slumbers the bat and the owl,
> And fierce beasts of prey were beginning to prowl.
>   Little bird, little bird, go to thy nest:
>   Thou art awake by day; now take thy rest.
>
> The huntresses came and they rode in their might.
> Some deer had they slain, and the rest took to flight;
> But one little fawn that an arrow laid low
> Crept away to a bush, so that no one should know.
>   Little bird, little bird, go to thy nest:
>   Thou art awake by day; now take thy rest.
>
> And yet some one had looked and had seen where it lay,
> For its mother had watched till the close of the day.
> Then, as the day closed and the darkness drew nigh,
> Crept down to the bush with a heart-rending sigh.
>   Little bird, little bird, go to thy nest:
>   Thou art awake by day; now take thy rest.
>
> Faint and weak lay her darling, still panting for breath:
> On its brow seemed to gather the damp dew of death.
> 'Oh! could I,' she thought, 'but some nourishment give,
> The wound still might heal, and my little one live.'
>   Little bird, little bird, go to thy nest:
>   Thou art awake by day; now take thy rest.
>
> Poor mother, poor mother! thy effort is vain!
> The dart in its flesh, and benumbed with the pain,

>   The fawn bleated sadly, and said with its eyes
>   ' Fain life would I drink, but I cannot arise.'
>   Little bird, little bird, go to thy nest :
>   Thou art awake by day; now take thy rest.
>
>   Yet cheer up, poor mother! the darkness has passed,
>   And thy poor little fawn finds a haven at last.
>   A huntress has carried it home in her breast,
>   Where it nestles secure and serene in its rest.
>   Little bird, little bird, go to thy nest :
>   Thou art awake by day ; now take thy rest."

"A place of peace, indeed, next thy heart, my Diláram," said Sheereen when the song was ended, and the girls, who had gathered together to hear it, were loud in their applause.

Meanwhile, Shápur had been sorely puzzled to know how to proceed. He had heard terrific tales of the fearful vengeance Maheen Bánoo and her tribe would wreak on any man who dared to intrude on their privacy, and consequently was not over-anxious to venture among them till he had made some trial of their temper. At last he bethought himself of trying the effect of Prince Khusroo's likeness on them, and fastened on a tree within their view one of several portraits of him drawn on white silk that he had brought with him. No sooner had Sheereen seen it than she directed one of her maidens to go and see what it was. The girl, finding it to be the portrait of a very handsome young man, feared the effect it might have on one of her mistress's excitable temperament, and, tearing it in pieces, returned with the intelligence that it had been merely an illusion which some demon who had a spite against them had put up on the tree to annoy them, and had vanished when she tried to take hold of it. Duly impressed with the power of magic from many things she had seen Maheen Bánoo do, Sheereen was satisfied with the explanation, and Shápur, finding his experiment a failure, made the best of his way back to the hermit's cave, determined to entrust him with the secret of his errand, and endeavour to gain his assistance in carrying it out. The long day drew gradually to an end, or, in Persian phraseology, the Ankâ (a fabulous bird supposed to live in the sun) sought his nest in the west, and Sheereen and her seventy companions mounted their horses and returned for the night to Maheen Bánoo's headquarters' camp.

CHAPTER IV.

THE RIDE ACROSS THE DESERT.

"FRIEND!" said the hermit, as Shápur entered the cave on his return, "the harvest of thy hope has been blasted by the autumn wind of disappointment."

"Thy words are true, O man of discernment," he answered; "but how knewest thou this? Has the bird of the woods whispered into the ear of thy sense what none could have known but thy slave?"

"He who lives in the corner of retirement," the hermit said, "and ponders on the things of the hidden world, hath his ears open to many voices inaudible by him whose ears are stopped with the wax of the affairs of this perishable existence. Lo, I touch thy forehead" (and he did so) "with the finger of penetration, and know that thou didst hang a picture on the tree, laying it as the grain of the fowler in thy snare before the pigeon of thy desire; but thy net was cut by the envious mouse of thy ill fortune, and the corn reached not the crop of that incautious bird. But though thy arrow has not yet struck the target of thy wish, the wheel of fortune still revolves, and the man of determination will never despair of an opportunity to try once more the strength of the bow of his purpose and the accuracy of the aim of his intent."

"The hands of my imagination are tied with the cords of ignorance," Shápur remarked. "Oh, let a ray from the sun of thy contrivance illumine the darkness of my helplessness, and light up for me the path of success!"

"Open, then, the lips of thy hope," then cheerfully said the hermit, "and thou shalt drink the wine of thy expectation. I will enchant the picture, so that it shall become the amber that shall attract the straw of Sheereen's desire. Hast thou another picture prepared?"

Shápur soon produced a facsimile of the prince's likeness that had been torn up the day before. This the hermit placed on the ground in the entrance of the cave, and drew round it a circle with his rod. On the circle he placed some of the dry thorns of which a heap was stored outside the cave, and setting them on fire waved his rod backwards and forwards over the picture with his right hand, while, muttering certain cabalistic sentences, he threw salt on the flames and made them flare up and crackle. Then, having sprinkled the embers with water from a cup over which he uttered more words of enchantment, he gave the portrait to Shápur again, saying:

"Go again in the morning to the new encampment of those fairy-faced ones, and hang it on a tree as thou didst to-day, and it shall come to pass that as soon as the eye of thy pigeon shall light upon it, the spark of desire shall light up in her soul the fire of love, which shall not be extinguished but with the water of union. But now eat the meagre food a hermit's store can alone afford thee, and rest on thy couch of grass till the herald of the army of the day terrifies the host of the moon and stars, and they withdraw themselves within the skirt of his garment of flame. God be thy protector!"

The lark had not shaken the dew off its wings for its first morning flight into the regions of the upper air when Shápur was on his way to the maidens' next day's bivouac, which they could reach by a shorter route than the rather circuitous one he had to follow among the hills. Their place of amusement was very similar to that of the previous day, but was rather more extensive.

The bevy of fair maidens were employed in their usual tasks and amusements when Shápur's picture again appeared. Of course it at once attracted Sheereen's attention. He had not managed on this occasion to put it up without being himself seen. Intensely excited, she sent one of her attendants to inquire who he was, and why he had put up the picture so mysteriously. He replied, saying to himself, "The seed has germinated, and if fate is propitious to Khusroo, it will grow into a goodly tree." Then aloud to the messenger, "Here is a pearl that is not to be threaded; and if it is, its method cannot be openly shown."

The words were repeated to Sheereen who, more and still more excited, went and sat by his side. He kissed the ground at her feet and praised her beauty, but at first gave no direct answer to her question of who he was and whence he came. He excited her curiosity by merely saying he was a man who had seen much good and much evil, and God had concealed from him no secrets either in the depths or in the heights. When she at last pressed him as to the significance of the picture, he promised to tell her in private if she would send away her attendants. These, who had clustered round their moon as the Pleiades, in Persian phrase, at a signal from their mistress scattered like stars in the Great Bear, and passed out of earshot. Shápur then told her the likeness was that of Khusroo Purweez, whose praises he proceeded to sing. He said of him that he was gentle as a deer, but in his rage like the fierce lion, a rose unwithered by the autumn's blast, a fresh-sprouting spring on the branch of youth, the leaf of whose water-lily had not yet appeared above the surface of the water, whose sun was as yet unobscured by a cloud, who would open a hundred doors with one breath from Paradise, whose mouth shed pearls as he spoke, at the drawing of whose sword the lion despaired of life, in descent sprung from Jumsheed, in dignity like the sun, before whose steed the world found the road narrow, who had raised his flag above the seven thrones, who intoxicated the ocean with its aroma when he took in his hand the cup of Kaikhusro, and who with all this magnificence and these virtues loved her to distraction, neither sleeping at night for seeing her image in his dreams, nor reposing by day from thinking of her.

The Persian chronicle relates that, overwhelmed with the description, Sheereen replied:

"Who is my friend in this whirlpool of trouble? The waters have passed over my head; what shall I do? I have no confidante among my companions. I am swallowed up in grief, and my heart has fallen. I am like a sick ass in the mud. This grief has penetrated my heart, and made my body like a withered narcissus."

Shápur answered: "O envy of the sun! May thy heart be soothed and thy life be prolonged! Since thy barque has fallen into this whirlpool, guide it to the shore again. Breathe not a word of this to any one; but pretend to-morrow to go to the chase. Mount Khusroo's horse Shubdeez and fly. None will reach him in the race. I give thee a ring of Khusroo's. Take it and go to his palace, where thou shalt find shelter among his female attendants until the prince comes, and thou mayest raise his throne from the earth to the heavens. Shubdeez shall go to Maheen Bánoo's camp to-night, and when thou mountest on his back in the morning, thou hast only to whisper the name of Khusroo in his ear for him to be thy slave until death."

Sheereen nodded her assent and went to her maidens, whose curiosity in endeavouring to find out what had passed between her and the strange man she had some difficulty in putting aside, and Shápur returned to the hermit's cave to tell him of his success and arrange for sending Shubdeez to Maheen Bánoo's camp.

The next morning's dawn saw Sheereen and her seventy attendants on their way to a favourite hunting-ground, where game was abundant. She had kept her counsel to herself, and no one had the slightest idea when she rode off at full speed after a buck that there was anything unusual in the proceeding. Her horse, it had been noticed, seemed particularly fresh and difficult to manage; but she was such a splendid horsewoman that her being apparently run away with caused no anxiety to her attendants, who believed the animal would soon tire himself out and be brought back subdued and tame. He had headed direct for the hills in the east, which were at no great distance, and, getting among the low forest at their base, was soon lost to sight. Sheereen then slackened his speed, so as not to waste his strength, and rode steadily on for several hours towards a place where she and her company had made their bivouac not long before, and where she knew there was water and grass. It was midday when she arrived there, and, turning Shubdeez loose to graze, laid herself down on the bank of a stream to think over her situation. Solitary as she found herself, she in no way repented of her undertaking. The handsome face she had seen in Shápur's picture, backed by his glowing description of the prince's excellencies, exercised that fascination over her mind which the hermit would fain have set down to his magical skill. There could be no doubt that he possessed in a great degree that power of influencing the wills of others, even at a distance, which in modern days has been called "mesmerism," or "electro-biology." Being looked upon as a holy man, he was consulted by members of all the nomad tribes in his own neighbourhood on matters of importance, and had thus had opportunities of becoming acquainted with Sheereen, of which he had not informed Shápur. He was intimately acquainted also with Maheen Bánoo, and assisted her in the taking of auguries and in other ceremonial observances enjoined by the custom of her tribe. He was in some degree, however, her rival in the profession of magic, and was not sorry on the present occasion to have it in his power to twit her with the failure of her celebrated mirror to foretell the coming event. We shall hear more of the hermit and his powers hereafter, but we must in the meanwhile follow Sheereen and her fortunes.

Riding on in the afternoon, and coming on a well-known track, she made for the encampment of a friendly tribe at the foot of the hills on the opposite side to the one she had entered by. Here she unhesitatingly rode up to the chief's tent, and announcing herself as Maheen Bánoo's niece, was hospitably entertained. For being alone and coming in so unceremonious a fashion, she made the excuse that she had had a quarrel with her aunt, and thought it advisable to visit her father's tribe for a time until their mutual anger had softened down. Her arrival in the camp caused considerable excitement, especially among the younger men, for her beauty was celebrated; and as she was well provided for among the chief's family, and the ormer could not pay her all the gallant little attentions one and all were eager to pay, they lavished them upon her horse, of whose good qualities, being themselves keen connoisseurs, they could not speak sufficiently highly. Shubdeez was thus in clover, and with good food and a night's rest was fresh for his next day's journey. That journey was to be for the most part over a sandy desert plain. Sheereen's host provided her, however, with some unleavened cakes and a bottle of mare's milk, and a bag of grain tied round his neck for Shubdeez. Many of the younger members of this wild tribe offered to escort her, but none of the offers were accepted. She told them that she was determined to go alone, and alone she departed.

It was a very trying journey for that lonely beautiful girl. Within an hour of sunrise the salt incrustation on the plain over which she was riding produced that perfect mirage which magnifies every stunted and thorny bush into a perfect tree, and reflects the image of every wild animal standing on the plain as perfectly as if the animal were standing alone on the brink of some placid lake. Onward and onward Sheereen the beautiful . and the courageous rode. Shubdeez was thirsty; but whenever he approached what he thought to be water it turned out to be only the idle desert mirage.

By midday even Shubdeez was faint and tired.

That was quite evident. Overpowered by the burning heat of the sun, and parched by thirst, Sheereen's proud spirit began to give way. Suddenly, as she rode over a rising piece of ground, she saw an oasis in the desert. Before her lay at no great distance a considerable stretch of water surrounded for some distance by greensward. This at any rate was no mirage. It was pure water bubbling up from a spring filling a small basin, and overflowing into a stream, which, before it was lost in the desert, was fringed for some distance with yellow blossoming acacias and pink oleanders. Imagine the joy such a discovery as this was to the wild beauty and her famous steed. It did not need her caressing touch to make him bound onwards to the water. Sheereen, like the horse, hastened to that fountain of life. She looked round to see that there was no one in sight, then she slipped off her outer garments and plunged into that delicious flood.

CHAPTER V.

WHAT HAPPENED NEXT.

SHE was dressed in a short skirt which revealed rather than concealed the fair form it covered. Another glance around, and then, being quite sure that there was no one in sight, she slipped this garment off also and plunged into the deep water. The Persian chronicler says that from contact with that glittering body the water of life was darkened, the wild rose united with the water-lily, and when she dipped herself in the limpid element it was as if the ermine had rolled itself over the face of night.

And then something else occurred. It so happened that after Shápur had departed in search of Sheereen, being in a restless state of mind, Prince Khusroo started off on the same errand. He left word that if Sheereen arrived during his absence she was to be hospitably entertained; but he himself, he said, was going away on a hunting expedition. The next day but one after Shápur's departure he was off too, and on the very morning that Sheereen was taking her bath in that desert lake he happened to have his camp in the neighbourhood. Whilst it was being pitched, and things were being made ready for his reception, he rode out to survey the plain. It was not long before he suddenly came in sight of the water, and of course he immediately made for it. In that water Sheereen was at the moment washing her long black hair, while an equally black horse marvellously like his own was grazing quietly at the edge of the lake. Sheereen saw him in a moment. It was a very awkward situation.

A very awkward situation indeed. Instantly the wild beauty drew her long hair around her, like the prototype of Lady Godiva, as she was, so that it answered perfectly the purposes of a veil.

"Can this be Sheereen and my own horse Shubdeez?" mused the prince.

"Can this be Khusroo?" was the thought which flashed across Sheereen's mind.

He was almost rooted to the spot by the girl's entrancing beauty; but of course he could scarcely remain where he was. He retreated and looked away, so that the desert princess had an opportunity, not only to put on her garments, but also to mount her horse. She was in doubt whether it could be Khusroo; but there was an irresistible attraction which drew her towards him. It was a genuine case of love at first sight. Still she was pledged to Khusroo, and this might not be the man. It was impossible to serve two masters, or to worship at two shrines. In her doubt and her distress she mounted Shubdeez and flew away like the wind. Khusroo turned his head and she was gone. He had found the spring-time, but had gathered no fruit from it. He had seen the river, but had not moistened his lips. He had seen his rose in the morning, but alas! he had not plucked the flower.

He made every effort to overtake her.

"She must have been a Peri," he thought, "flying from the sight of a man, or she could not have become so suddenly invisible."

As it was useless to stay longer where he was, he marched out in the afternoon towards the hill of Armán. Sheereen rode onwards at full speed until she thought she was no longer pursued, and then she slackened Shubdeez' pace until they reached Khusroo's palace. It was a difficult position; but, then, she lived in the East and not in the West. She claimed admittance, and told the attendants that in time Khusroo himself would tell her story. She begged them in the meantime to attend to Shubdeez, who had indeed proved himself an animal of great price; naturally the attendants recognized the horse. Sheereen was received by the female attendants with all the honours that could be shown her. They clothed her in rich garments; and as she rested from the fatigues of her journey, then, to use the Persian phrase, the rose of union with Khusroo bloomed for her in the garden of promise.

The bride had come home before the bridegroom, for, meanwhile, Khusroo, having reached the confines of the kingdom, was royally entertained by the wardens of the marches. After some days of enjoyment he passed on to Khuzistán. Maheen Bánoo heard of his arrival. She was overwhelmed with grief because of the loss of her niece, who she thought must have been killed by some wild beast; but she came out in due state to meet Khusroo. She went through the usual *Istikbál*, or ceremony of greeting, and invited him to confer honour on Barora, her capital. Khusroo consented. If he had only known what he was missing! but, then, he thought he was near the prize.

Shápur appeared before long, and from him he heard the whole story of what had happened. Then Khusroo came to a very queer determination. He sent Shápur off on Sheereen's own horse Goolgoon, an animal almost the equal of Shubdeez, to fetch Sheereen back. On his arrival at the palace Sheereen was quite eager to return home. There she was received with great rejoicing by Maheen Bánoo and her attendants, who do not seem to have had any idea as to where she had been beyond this, that she had been lost on a hunting expedition.

The would-be lovers, however, had not yet come to the end of their troubles. Two days before her return a carrier had reached Khusroo with the news that his father, King Hormuz, was dead. His friends advised him strongly to take immediate possession of the throne of Persia. Love gave way to self-interest. Having done this, he gave a series of State entertainments, when in the course of hunting one day he came across Sheereen once more. Suddenly hearing a sweet voice singing, he stood still to listen, and this was the song :

> " I look down below, and I look up above ;—
> Tell me, O nightingale, where is my love?
> Fondly I search the horizon's bound,
> Say where, sweet bird, my love may be found.
>
> Oh! is he there in the sun's glorious light,
> Or in the moon's gentle radiance at night?
> Say, does he rest in the sea's cavern deep,
> Where the pearl in its mother-shell lieth asleep?
>
> With my bodily eye I cannot see him here,
> But the eye of my spirit still whispers, ' He's near.'
> Nightingale, mount to the bright sky above,
> Look down and tell me, oh! where is my love?"

It turned out to be one of the day bivouacs of Sheereen and her maidens. As he came forward from his hiding-place, the startled cry of "The prince! The prince!" from her attendants told Sheereen who her visitor was, and a glance showed her he was the same person whom she had seen as she sat in her *al fresco* bath. It needed no more to tell him Sheereen was before him. She, after the custom of her people, hastened to kiss the ground at his feet. To lift her up and kiss her hand was the work of a moment; but as the attendants on both sides ran to the spot a somewhat awkward pause ensued. Sheereen, however, with a deep blush that enhanced her charms, quickly ended it by saying, "The sky derives dignity from thy crown, and the earth loftiness from thy throne. Though thou hast a hundred thousand slaves better than I am, yet I have a dwelling-place in this neighbourhood which, if the king will honour by his presence, in binding her loins in thy service the head of thy servant will be exalted. If the elephant passes over the carpet of the ant, the robe of her who has fallen will fall into the blue!"* The invitation, of course, was eagerly accepted. Maheen Bánoo, on being informed of what had happened, sent a royal banquet, and he was soon installed in a palace shaded by trees like the Tooba of Paradise.

* That is, will be dyed and freshened up again.

CHAPTER VI.

THE PRINCESS'S WARNING, AND THE BEAUTY'S VOW.

MAHEEN BÁNOO was wise in her generation in knowing the feeling Sheereen entertained towards the prince; she bethought herself of the necessity of caution in leaving fuel and fire in close proximity to each other; she spoke seriously to her niece on the subject. She told her she was a sealed treasure; that she did not know the good and evil of the world, for it knew how to use fascination to steal a pearl or pierce a ruby. If this lord of the world had given his heart to her, she had hunted noble game; but she must turn a deaf ear to his blandishments and not yield to his impatience, for men, she said, were clever at all stratagems and deceit. For all his honeyed words, he must not be allowed to eat sweetmeats without cost, and she must not fall into his oven before she had eaten bread. As she was of pure disposition, she should act as an antidote to his poison, nor become as Vees with Rámeen. She must not scratch the face of her good name with dry thorns, but live with fair fame. She had heard that he had ten thousand sweet-lipped and chain-haired beauties at his command; and if his heart laughed at all these roses, how could she know that his affection would remain firm to one pearl? If he knew her purity and fair fame, he would ask for her with all honour. Sheereen was to remember that she was no lower than himself in rank, for had not Maheen Bánoo an ample kingdom? If he was a moon, she was a sun. If he was Káoos, she was Afrásiáb. She must not follow after men like Zuleikha, but be like Wámik's lover Uzrá; for there were many who threw away a rose after its first sweet scent had left it, and wine from the cup when they had once tasted it. If she would follow this advice, she would not fall into misfortune.

Sheereen, the chronicler relates, fastened these admonitions as a ring in her ear, and swore by the seven thrones of light, and by the glorious Testament of the Lord of the world, that if she had to weep tears of blood for it she would never be anything but Khusroo's lawful wife.

Some time was now passed by the lovers and their companions in feasting and sport. Not a day passed that Sheereen did not lead the way to some enchanting spot among the hills in the neighbourhood, or on the plain close to them, whence, when the chase had been unsuccessful, or she and her maidens were tired of hurling the "chogân," or throwing the spear—sports in which they rivalled the men of the prince's suite—they could retire into some shady place to pass the hotter hours of the day. Neither the song nor, unfortunately, the wine-cup were wanting in their feasts. There were, in addition to Sheereen herself, several in her company who were proficient on the barbut, or lute, and could on occasion improvise songs on the adventures of the day, and amongst the attendants of Khusroo some who had studied music under Bárbud, the famous singer, who shared with Nakisá the musical and poetical honours of the Persian court of the day. It was in an era previous to that in which the advent of the religion of the Arabian prophet, who no doubt was well aware of the excess to which wine-drinking was carried, especially among the nomad tribes, checked the propensity to indulgence, and endeavoured to put a stop to it by prohibiting the use of wine altogether. Women, as well as men, were given to it. We have said that the vice of intoxication had already led Khusroo into scrapes. This, however, had not cured him of the propensity; and although Sheereen by her own studied moderation set a good example, the custom of the country was such that she could not have abstained altogether, for fear of being counted wanting in the duties of hospitality. The scenes that took place at these festive meetings were therefore sometimes unpleasant. On one occasion a lion disturbed them. Its appearance was followed by an immediate stampede of those on the spot; but Khusroo, probably in one of his drunken fits, and foolhardy accordingly, went against it with a spear, and succeeded, possibly more by good luck than good management, in killing it. On his return from this adventure, with the dead animal borne before him in triumph to lay at Sheereen's feet, he first claimed for his reward permission to kiss her hand; but, not content with this, proceeded to kiss her lips, an operation to which she prudently submitted for the time being; but the incident, much as she loved him, fortified her in her determination that nothing should induce her to share his throne till his bad habit was conquered. When he had recovered himself, she warned him of the consequences, and pointed out the disgrace into which he was bringing the name of a Persian king, a descendant of such illustrious ancestors as Noushirwán and Kaikhusroo, darkening the sun of their glory with the eclipse of the moon of self-indulgence, and himself sinking from the height of the heaven of majesty into the gloomy sea of dishonour. She lectured him soundly. She told him he had already been absent a long time from his seat of government, and it was her duty to tell him to return, in spite of her fear that he might accuse her of a want of hospitality; for could he expect that his subjects, when the sun of their adoration was long hid from them by the fog of absence, would not turn their faces towards a moon illumining their night, unobscured by the clouds of doubt? Did he not remember that Behrám Choobeen had already spread a scandalous report that he had blinded his father, and on that account, as well as from his youth and inexperience, was unfit to rule over them?

On this entreaty Khusroo promised her that he would reform; but she must allow him for a few days more to enjoy the light of her presence and drink the wine of her beauty. Weakly she did not insist on his going away, and the few days of grace he had begged for became a week, and the week became a month. About this time alarming rumours began to be spread about that the people of Ajam were tired of waiting for their king, and were turning their eyes towards Behrám Choobeen, who was said to be returning from Russia, where he had taken refuge after his defeat by Khusroo. The infatuation of drink and Sheereen's presence still possessed Khusroo. He would not believe the bad news, and dallied on from day to day.

He was seated once on the bank of a stream, having just awoke from a heavy sleep, when his attention was drawn to a crowd in the camp. There was something unusual afoot, that was quite clear; and Khusroo arose in anger from his drunken sleep.

CHAPTER VII.

MOHAMMED'S EMISSARY.

TO us who only know Mohammedanism as a great power in the world, it is strange to read in the ancient Persian record how first Khusroo heard of the new religion. An old man with long, flowing, white beard and naked to the waist, holding in his left hand a rod of polished steel covered with iron rings, which he rattled as he came, advanced towards the camp. In his right hand was a paper, which he held to his head. Slowly he advanced towards Khusroo. In spite of the thronging of the people, he pressed onwards, looking neither to the right hand nor to the left, repeating always the now familiar formula, "There is no God but Allah, and Mohammed is His prophet; there is no God but Allah, and Mohammed is His prophet."

It was the hermit of the cave. The founder of Islam was at this time in his full career of conquest in Arabia; and having nearly subdued all his enemies he determined to send messengers to all the surrounding countries calling upon them to renounce Paganism and to embrace the worship of the true God. News travelled but slowly in those far-off days, and hardly anything was known in Persia of the advent of the prophet. The hermit had, however, heard of what was occurring, and he crossed over into Arabia to see for himself what was going on. The fiery zeal of the first followers of Mohammed found in him a kindred spirit. He was initiated in the new cult. He saw the prophet himself. Mohammed had intrusted him with a written document to Khusroo. The document he pressed against his forehead as he came forward boldly, and with none of those abject tokens of humility with which it was customary to approach the presence of Persian monarchs. The hermit respectfully kissed the document, and then he handed it to Khusroo, who with a gesture of impatience opened it. It was, however, written in Arabic, a language he did not understand. One of his attendants was better informed, and interpreted it to him.

This was the letter :

"From the Vicegerent of Allah the Merciful, the Compassionate, the Lord of the two worlds, the Giver of all that is good, and the Destroyer of all that is evil. Be it known to Khusroo, commonly known as Purweez, ruler of Ajam, that thou and thy subjects have gone astray in the wilderness of unbelief, and worship the sun and the moon and the hosts of heaven, which Allah has created and which are no gods. Wherefore turn ye and be converted, and abandon your vain imaginations and worship the one true God, Who has sent thee his slave to show you the way. Obey the word, and follow in the path. If you shall wander again, lo, the sword is drawn. Ye shall be rooted out of the earth, and cast into hell."

Khusroo could hardly bear with patience the reading of this mysterious scroll.

"Who is this dog of an Arab," he exclaimed, "who dares to tell us that we should abandon the faith of our fathers and follow after some new strange god?"

"There is no God but Allah, and Mohammed is the prophet of Allah," was the reply.

"We know," said Khusroo, angrily, "that the Christians have gods and the Greeks and Romans have gods; but who is Allah that we should serve him, and no longer look up to the light of heaven that gives us heat and warmth, the vapour and clouds, whence comes the rain that provides us with our meat and drink? And who is this dog that calls himself Mohammed and the prophet of God?"

"Thou blasphemest," said the hermit with bitter emphasis; "thou blasphemest the elect of Allah, and hast sealed thine own fate. Though for a time the white banner of victory float over thee as thou mountest higher and higher to the Damávend of fame, there shall come an hour when the rushing river of calamity shall bear thee down to the depths of woe. I have spoken."

Khusroo tore the letter to pieces, and throwing it into the stream at his feet, exclaimed:

"Seize the dog. Let him not depart hence. Seize him, and strike off his head."

Khusroo's followers rushed forward to execute their

lord's commands, which would have been carried out to the letter had not Sheereen's maidens, who had collected together to see what was the cause of the disturbance, closed round him. The hermit, taking advantage of the succour thus brought him, walked proudly away, saying, " Allahu akbar ! God is great ! There is but one God, and Mohammed is His prophet !"

CHAPTER VIII.

KHUSROO GETS MARRIED, AND THEN FIGHTS A GREAT BATTLE.

THE blow was not long in falling. Messenger after messenger soon arrived with the news that the people, disgusted with the continued absence of their king, and not knowing to whom to turn in the hour of their need when the near approach of Behrám Choobeen, with a large army of Tartars, the daughter of whose chief he was reported to have married, was announced, would certainly declare for him. Forced at last out of his apathy by the news, backed up by the entreaties of Maheen Bánoo and Sheereen, Khusroo turned towards his capital, Madáin. About a day's march from it he was met by an officer of some rank in Behrám's army, who bore a letter couched in the most offensive and haughty terms. Styling himself the friend of the gods, the conqueror of men and satrap of satraps, the enemy of tyrants, the general of the armies of Persia, and a prince adorned with the title of eleven virtues, he called on Khusroo to shun the example of his father and avoid his fate, to imprison those traitors who had been released from their chains, to deposit in some holy place the diadem which he had usurped, and accept from his gracious benefactor pardon for his faults and the government of a province. Greatly incensed at the insolence of the message, Khusroo would have ordered the immediate execution of the messenger had he not been over-persuaded by those about him, and warned of the disgrace that would fall upon him if he took the life of an ambassador. He therefore contented himself with refusing to allow him to return to the camp of his master, and kept him in attendance on himself while he pushed on with all speed.

Arrived at Madáin, he found everything in confusion —that of course—and the people of the city in consternation at the news that the Tartar army was but a single march off. With difficulty he persuaded the townspeople to take up arms in their own defence, by pointing out to them the horrors that would certainly result from an invasion of the nomad savages, and with the former, and the slaves of the palace hastily equipped for the occasion, marched out to meet the rebellious general. What might have been expected occurred: Khusroo's small force found itself many times out-numbered, and, awed by the martial appearance of the masses of cavalry with which Behrám advanced, turned to escape at the first flight of arrows shot among them. In vain was Khusroo's personal bravery, in vain his appeals to the people to strike a blow for the sanctity of their homes and the honour of their wives and daughters; they threw away their weapons and fled back to the city. Astonished at the smallness of the numbers opposing him, and fearing an ambuscade, Behrám followed cautiously, but found the gates open and Khusroo himself fled. He had gone off at once, escorted by but a few followers, and attended by his own immediate household. They were followed in hot haste by Tartar horse sent in pursuit by Behrám; but having a whole day's start, and being better acquainted with the country than their pursuers, they gained the mountainous country held by Maheen Bánoo and her tribe without molestation. Here, split up into small parties, and smuggled through the hills by different paths known only to themselves by the friendly nomads, they gained so much on their enemies that their farther pursuit was considered useless, and was abandoned.

Khusroo had now before him the choice of two alternatives: to lurk in hiding among the nomads, or to implore the assistance of the emperor at Constantinople. He loved Sheereen, and wished to take the former course; but he knew that Maheen Bánoo and her tribe could be but of little assistance to him in his endeavour to retrieve his fortunes and regain the throne of his ancestors, whereas if the emperor helped him he might hope for the assistance of the power of Greece. Led by his early training in the religion of Zoroaster to a superstitious belief in auguries, he determined to allow the matter to decide itself by chance, and as he arrived in the open country beyond the hills he threw the reins on the neck of his horse. Shubdeez, probably guided by his natural instinct in the direction of water, took the road towards the Euphrates, and this determined Khusroo's fate. He made up his mind to implore the aid of the Emperor Maurice, into whose territory he accordingly crossed. Traversing the desert on the other bank of the river, he halted not far from Circesium, then held by a Greek garrison, and sent on word of his arrival to the prefect. That officer admitted him to the fortress, and subsequently forwarded him with befitting ceremony to Hierapolis. Thence the fugitive king sent an embassy to Constantinople, and awaited its return. The letter sent to the emperor referred to the vicissitudes of fortune, and the common interests of princes. It set forth in severe terms the ingratitude of Behrám, and it urged that it would be to the advantage of the Greeks to support the two great monarchies of the world, the two great luminaries by whose salutary influence it was vivified and adorned. In reply to this representation the emperor assured him that he would espouse the cause of justice and royalty; that he would not invite Khusroo to Constantinople on account of the expense and delay of such a visit; but in token of good-will sent him jewels and gold and a valuable diadem. The best proof of his favour, however, lay in his directing Narses, his general, to assemble a powerful army on the borders of Syria and Armenia, and, crossing the Euphrates, not to sheath his sword until he had restored Khusroo to his throne. The emperor at the same time gave him his daughter Miriam in marriage.

Having obtained the military assistance he required, Khusroo lost no time in marching directly on Madáin, carrying with him his new wife Miriam, who was a Christian. Willingly as the people of Persia had in the first instance consented to the expulsion of the ancient dynasty of the Sassânian kings and the assumption of the throne by Behrám Choobeen, the priests had refused to consecrate him, and he had thus been forced to assume the sceptre by force. The people, as a rule, had soon repented of their precipitancy in not supporting the grandson of their great king Noushirwán, and the son of Hormuz, and the executions of individuals and other severities with which Behrám endeavoured to consolidate his power had only the effect of irritating them, so that when it became known that their legitimate king was coming to assert his rights with the assistance of a Greek army the revulsion of feeling was complete, and showed itself by numbers of partisans flocking to his standards as soon as he entered the country. All along his route his march was left unimpeded, for Behrám was afraid to leave the treacherous population of the capital city in his rear, and he determined to risk all on the issue of a single battle before the walls of Madáin itself. The total force he had been able to collect together were about forty thousand, the Tartars having in the meanwhile returned to their own homes, while the king's army numbered about sixty thousand.

Behrám had made a skilful disposition of his troops,

in order to make up for his inferiority in strength. His rear rested on the walls of the city, so that he could not be attacked from behind; and on each side was a mound where were situated two dokhmás, or towers, for the exposure of the dead to be devoured by birds of prey, according to the practice of fire-worshippers, to prevent being taken in flank. The front was thus the only side on which his army was exposed, and even this was partly protected by the watercourses that irrigated the fruit and vegetable gardens of the city. If there was any fault to be found with the position, it was that the front did not leave sufficient room for the deploying of the troops.

Khusroo and the Greek commander had halted their troops on the previous night about two miles outside the town, in order to give them the advantage of a night's rest after the fatigue of crossing the desert. The angel of darkness had hardly commenced to lift up his skirt to allow the passage of the advanced guard of the army of light, in other words, the day had hardly begun to dawn, when they moved forward. In the centre were the Greeks, numbering about forty thousand, drawn up in two lines according to their cohorts, in double ranks. They were ordered to use their shields as a protection against arrows, until they came to close quarters, by the men in front carrying theirs in a position to cover their bodies as much as possible, and those in the rear rank holding theirs over the heads both of the front rank men and themselves. The right wing, commanded by Khusroo in person, consisted of his personal followers, and others who had joined him *en route*, having men on foot in the centre and a few horsemen on each side. On the left, Shápur, who had faithfully adhered to his friend and master's fortunes, commanded, having the same disposition on his side as the king had on the right. The centre, it had been arranged, should be held back and kept out of sight as much as possible, in order to allow the two wings to execute a manœuvre which, it was hoped, would induce the enemy to come forward and deprive him of the advantage of his position. Accordingly, in the advance the right wing was somewhat confused, and Shápur led on his troops apparently rather hurriedly and in an irregular manner, as if anxious to be the first to come into action. He knew every inch of the ground, however, and made straight for the point where he was aware that the watercourses were most numerous and difficult to cross. Here, in apparent perplexity, his men stood and commenced to discharge arrows at their opponents. The manœuvre succeeded. One of Behrám's officers, thinking the opportunity of taking the enemy at a disadvantage was one not to be lost, drew out his men from the centre, and vigorously attacked those of Shápur's left wing. Now was Khusroo's opportunity. Quickly wheeling the cavalry of his wing to the left, he struck in in front of the advancing Greeks, with a view to assist Shápur and throw the enemy in his turn into confusion. But Behrám was too wary a general to allow this without an effort to parry the stroke. Leading his men forward in person, he attacked Khusroo's wing in flank as it moved across his front; a hand to hand engagement took place, and as the Greeks had by this time come forward, the battle became general. The Greek cohorts pressed forward steadily and persistently. Khusroo on one side and Behrám on the other were in the thickest of the fight, and in striving to get at each other performed prodigies of valour, but were prevented meeting by the crush of combatants. The dust stirred by the feet of men and horses and the never-ceasing flights of arrows combined to darken the air. The whizzing of missiles, the clashing of swords and spears, the screams of horses, the battle-cries and shouts of men, and the groans and shrieks of the wounded, were indescribable.

The roaring of the drums gave ears to the dead, and deprived the living of their senses : in that forest the wild ass escaped not from the raging lion, nor the lion from the devouring of the sword; the horsemen had drawn their lightning-flashing swords, and the fierce ones had bared their teeth one upon another; death lurked in ambush for life, and the spear prepared the day of judgment for the world ; the eagles had mixed their arrows with blood, and royal decrees rested upon the feathers of the vultures; the red silk of the banners was opened out, and the sugar-cane field burnt up with fire.

Behrám's troops had now all pressed forward from between the two hillocks. The battle was at its fiercest, when above the noise of the combat there were heard the clatter as of a thousand horses' hoofs, and the shrill sound of women's voices singing:

> " Ride, sisters, ride,
> On your swift steeds of pride ;
> See that our women's arms strike for the right !
> Now with the lightning's flash
> Straight through the foe we dash,
> On till he saves himself headlong in flight ! "

And with cries of "Maheen, Maheen! Sheereen, Sheereen!" Maheen Bánoo's tribe, with Sheereen and her seventy maidens at their head, galloped over the hillock to the right into the rear of Behrám's men and charged them home. Behrám himself saw further resistance was hopeless, and fled to his father-in-law's tribe. His men trampled each other to death in irretrievable confusion, and the Greek cohorts marched steadily on through the wounded and dead into the gates of the city.

CHAPTER IX.

KHUSROO AND HIS WIFE CONVERSE.

ONCE again Khusroo entered into the palace of his ancestors in triumph and amid the acclamations of his people, who, disgusted with the recent severity of Behrám, and recollecting that the faults of the former had been faults of omission rather than of commission, of youthful heedlessness rather than of deliberate neglect, welcomed the return of their sovereign as the recommencement of an era of peace and prosperity. The city rejoiced, and its inhabitants testified their satisfaction and thankfulness to the army, and especially to the foreign soldiers, by whom the victory had been achieved, by welcome gifts of supplies of food and wine, to which the troops had of late been unaccustomed. Preparations were at once commenced for a grand banquet in the king's palace that evening, to which all the leading Greek officers were to be invited. Nor were the humbler members of the population forgotten amid the general rejoicings, for Khusroo ordered the royal treasury to be opened and abundant *largesse* to be bestowed upon the poor.

Immediately after the battle, Sheereen and her tribe had disappeared as suddenly as they had come, so suddenly that Khusroo, anxious to thank her for the signal assistance she had rendered him, had been unable to do so. As a sovereign he owed her a deep debt of gratitude for the timely aid given at a crisis in his fortunes, and his heart was stirred with the liveliest emotion towards one who had fearlessly exposed her own life to danger for his sake. He would have ridden off on the spot in pursuit of her, if the prudent counsel of Shápur that on such an occasion his presence in person was due to his people had not restrained him, and induced him to content himself with sending off a messenger to express his thanks verbally. He begged her to accept his hospitality, and honour with her presence the royal banquet that was to take place in the evening. He did not leave the field without directing the immediate despatch to the camp of the tribe, wherever it might be, of ample supplies for them and green fodder for their horses. The latter was grown abundantly in the gardens that surrounded the city.

The *cortège* that escorted Queen Miriam had followed closely in the march of the army, and she was able to take part in her husband's triumphal procession to the palace. The procession was on a scale of true Oriental magnificence. Headed by a band of drummers beating the long brass drum called "koos," of a deep bass tone, interspersed with others playing on highly pitched kettle-drums, the two sets of instruments, keeping exact time with each other, produced a rude kind of monotonous, though rhythmical, melody which enabled the troops to swing along with a martial, even-paced step, sadly disturbed by the occasional interludes of the band of musicians blowing upon the "nai," a reed instrument, with a note resembling that of the Scotch bagpipes, who followed close behind them. Then came a tribe of nomad Tartars, with long hair curled in ringlets, armed with shield and spear, and with bows and quivers of arrows slung over their shoulders, whose dirty and ragged appearance added in the eyes of the peaceable inhabitants of the city to the savageness of their demeanour. Next there followed a troop of twenty elephants with highly ornamented cloths of gold beneath howdahs painted in brilliant colours, on which were seated the officers of the Greek and native troops. The docile but unwieldy beasts at the command of their drivers repeatedly raised their trunks in salutation and uttered their shrill, trumpet-like cries, and added to the Babel-like confusion of sounds that accompanied the shouts of the populace, and their exclamations of, "May his life be prolonged!" "May his good fortune endure!" "May his prosperity endure for ever!" "May the rising sun of his reign soon reach the meridian of sovereignty!" and other Oriental expressions of good-will. Following the elephants were fifty highly caparisoned camels bearing takht-i-rawân, or travelling litters, in which were seated, evidently very uncomfortable from the swinging motion they had to put up with, the female attendants of Queen Miriam, the foreigners among whom attracted the special attention of the people of the country. In their midst was the queen herself, in a litter drawn by a pure white Bactrian dromedary of easy paces, pale and languid from fatigue, and yet upholding by her high mien and lofty bearing the dignity due to a daughter of the Emperor of Rome. Her appearance was hailed by the populace with renewed shouts of, " May the queen live for ever!" "The moon moving gracefully among the Pleiades shall never suffer the disgrace of eclipse!" many of them prostrating themselves and touching the ground with their foreheads in salutation and homage.

If the enthusiasm of the people was great as the queen passed, it was redoubled when, after the march of a cohort of Greek troops behind her, Khusroo himself came by. He was dressed from head to foot in chain armour inlaid with gold, and seated on his favourite horse Shubdeez, which was also clothed over head, neck, and shoulders with similar armour. He carried in his right hand a battle-axe, its polished blade glittering in the sun. As he rode slowly by, the frantic citizens were only prevented by the whips of his attendants on foot, and which were used without mercy, from throwing themselves under his horse's hoofs. Shápur, in chain armour, but little less gorgeous than that of the king, followed on horseback a few paces behind on his right, and the Greek general, in knight's armour, in a similar position on his left hand. Behind them came, surrounding the royal standard-bearer, carrying aloft on his spear's point the long milk-white horse's tail that Khusroo had adopted for his banner, a large number of the nobles of the court, also on horseback and in armour. These were followed by more richly caparisoned elephants, and the rear was brought up by detachments of the army, native and foreign troops alternating with each other.

This spectacle of barbaric splendour, supported, as it was, by the solid masses of the Greek troops, was well fitted to make a deep impression on the minds of the white-robed multitudes, who not only thronged the streets through which the procession passed, but crowded the flat roofs of the houses on each side. This feeling was intensified as Khusroo arrived before the principal fire-temple of the city, in front of which stood the chief Mobed. He was clothed in white and wore a long white beard, with his hands upraised in the attitude of blessing. Khusroo got off his horse and prostrated himself at the old man's feet. This was all that was wanted to enlist the hearts of the beholders, and the fervent cries of "Khoodá háfiz!" "God protect you!" raised on all sides convinced the king that at all events for the time being he had the people thoroughly on his side.

And yet Khusroo was sad, for she who was the light of his eyes and the life of his soul was not present to share his triumph. He had married Miriam, as it may be supposed, more as a matter of policy than as one of affection, in order to secure the emperor's assistance in recovering his throne from the usurpation of Behrám. He had conformed to the usages of the age in visiting her and assiduously paying her all due ceremonious attention. Enervated by the habit of drinking heavily which he had acquired, and surrounded by other evil influences of an Oriental court he yet preserved in his hand one spot green—the memory of his beloved Sheereen. With any real affection for Miriam not only did this passion interfere, but the difference in their religions, she being a Christian, prevented the springing up of common sentiments and mutual sympathy that might by degrees have led to love. With regard to Sheereen, his devotion had by the morning's incident been intensified by gratitude, and yearning for her presence, he determined to strike whilst the iron was hot and broach the matter to Miriam. Having married a Christian, he had, by a formal stipulation to that effect, in a manner bound himself to respect the feelings of herself and her co-religionists in the matter of not having more than one wife; but he determined to endeavour to overcome her objection to his marriage with Sheereen. Accordingly, only allowing the queen time to rest herself a little after the excitement and fatigue of the early part of the day, he sought her apartment in the afternoon, and after enlarging on the great obligation they were both under to Sheereen for her conduct in the battle, and the political advantage of bringing her warlike tribe, whose dwelling-place lay in the direct path of enemies coming from the West, under the immediate rule of Persia, he suggested the advisability of making Sheereen his second wife, of course in a position inferior in the royal household to that of his chief queen. He took care to base his proposition on these grounds alone, avoiding all allusion to her beauty and accomplishments, and studiously concealing his former acquaintance with her. He urged that, although the practice of monogamy had been adopted by those of the Christian faith, it was under no express commandment from its Founder, and the great patriarchs, from Abraham downwards to David and Solomon, had had more than one wife. Miriam had, however, heard the story of his long absence in the camp of the nomads, and the neglect of the affairs of his kingdom that had paved the way for the usurpation of the throne by Behrám Choobeen, and shrewdly surmised the state of Khusroo's feelings towards the nomad queen. She listened silently to him to the end of his speech, and then firmly and decisively refused her consent. Knowing that he had only married her as a matter of policy, and not from any attachment to herself personally, she was well aware that the coming between them of one to whom her husband was under such a great obligation could only tend to estrange him from her more than ever, and banish all chance of the fulfilment of the hope that with the birth of the child she was soon to bear to him he might be drawn towards her. The answer was therefore brief and decisively in the negative, and she gave him clearly to understand that if in the exercise of his sovereign power he disregarded her wishes, she would not hesitate to put an end to her own existence. Obviously this was plain speaking.

CHAPTER X.

THE HERMIT ONCE MORE.

IN the evening the city was illuminated in Oriental style. The illumination was carried out by means of earthenware saucers filled with naptha, derived from wells on the shores of the Caspian Sea, the illuminating powers of the oil being already known and taken advantage of in the neighbouring countries. The outlines of the houses, and of their windows and archways, were picked out with these saucers suspended on strings, and in all public open spaces, and especially in the vicinity of the palace; similar saucers were arranged on the ground in various flower and geometrical patterns, shedding a gentle halo of light over the whole city. There was hardly a breath of air stirring, so that the effect of the illumination was kept up all the night by the saucers being constantly replenished with naptha. The banquet which followed was a right royal one. All the nobles of the court, and the principal officers of both the foreign and native troops, the most prominent citizens, and the chiefs of the nomad tribes within convenient distance of the capital, attended, clothed in their most sumptuous apparel. On a raised daïs in the centre of the great throne-room of the palace was placed the celebrated throne of Khusroo, for the use of himself and his queen. This is said to have been of pure gold, and to have been adorned by a thousand globes of gold representing the planets and the constellations of the Zodiac. The hall itself was of great height, and so large that the roof had to be supported by forty thousand pillars of silver of various orders of architecture. During the banquet bands of musical instruments played in the adjoining courts; and as soon as the serious part of the entertainment was over, and the wine cup circulated freely around, dancing women exhibited their skill in singing and posturing after the manner of the East. In addition to the flesh of domesticated beasts, venison and birds, such as the partridge and woodcock, the sand-grouse and aquatic birds, and fruits such as the orange, the apple, and the pomegranate, played a conspicuous part. After some time it became unequivocally clear that with regard to many who were present the limits of rational enjoyment had been passed. But before this point had been reached, the queen had withdrawn, and Khusroo was left to occupy the throne alone. He had drunk heavily, and was, in fact, rapidly becoming intoxicated, when he was instantaneously brought to his senses by a cry at the entrance of the hall, in the stentorian voice of the hermit of the cave, of, "Lá hául wa là koowut illá b' illáh! There is no virtue nor power but in Allah!"

As the words were uttered, the hermit walked with slow and deliberate step, unhindered by the attendants or guests, up to the centre of the hall to the king's throne. Khusroo started from his seat in anger, and was about to speak, when, apparently reduced to helplessness by the action of the hermit in fixing his eye and pointing his finger at his forehead, he sank back, and listened as the old man went on:

"There is no God but Allah, and Mohammed is the messenger of Allah! Hear, O ye wine-bibbers and gluttons, and open your ears, O ye worshippers of fire! Is it to see ye wallowing in the filth of your appetites, like the unclean beast, that I have left the corner of seclusion to come into the desert of the world? Is it to inflame my senses with the juice of the grape till I become as devoid of wisdom as the beasts of the field that I come, eating by the way the parched grain of weariness and drinking the muddy water of pain? Nay, but to bring ye back from the path of error in which ye walk, and to illuminate your road with the lantern of truth! Lo! this is the message I bring you from the prophet of God, in the name of the King who is without life, and without whom is no life; the Ancient One who has no rising, and the Great One whose ending is not ordained; the Creator of being, who can destroy an elephant by means of a gnat, or save a prophet through an ant. To Him make thy supplications, though thou mayest be great, for if He throw into hell every devout man who is on the earth His decree is proper, and if every sad sinner He bring into Paradise He is not wrong. Though thou rulest, power is of God. Seek not to know the 'what' and 'how much,' for the servant is in the hand of his lord. For lordship God alone is fit: it does not become a servant. Thou art but a created thing, who in the end must die. When wilt thou deliver thyself from the hand of death? Look not to thyself, for he who relies on himself has no sight. The earth revolves from His creation, and of Him are the four quarters of the world. Reflect on what is greater in thy kingdom than the honouring of God, and bear witness that the Creator is one God. He is not in a certain place, and He requires no fixed abode. God, who has given rule to man, has made Mohammed His messenger to man. Turn ye from the worship of fire, and make a Paradise of the law to escape from hell. Delight ye yourselves like peacocks in this garden; and like the moth save yourselves from the stain of fire, by becoming Mussulmans. 'Allahu Akbar!' 'God is greatest!'"

During this speech, the king sat apparently stupefied and under the influence of the hermit's power. When the hermit ended, he looked, as if for assistance, to the Chief Priest, who sat not far from the throne, and the latter rose from his seat amid suppressed signs of encouragement from the rest of the company. Addressing the hermit, he said with an air of dignity and patience that well became his sacred office and personal appearance:

"Friend, I see that thy newly kindled fanaticism has in some degree upset the balance of thy understanding and weighed down the scale towards the side of presumption and insolence; otherwise thou wouldest not have come in this guise before the King of kings."

"I know of no King of kings," fiercely interrupted the hermit, "but Allah. He is the King of kings!"

"Friend," continued the Mobed, calmly, "thou knowest well that the title refers to earthly and not to heavenly dignities. There is but one King of kings and Lord of lords who, as thou sayest, is the Creator of all things, and whom, being invisible to mortal eye, we worship through His visible emblems, the sun that warms and vivifies all creation, the moon and the planets and the host of heaven, which illumine the night, and by their combinations or oppositions in their various spheres foretell, if they do not order and control, the actions of men. We acknowledge but one God, as thou thyself dost, in Asura Majda, the Great Spirit. Him thou callest Allah, and the patriarchs of the Jews worshipped under the name of Jehovah. What difference is there between us? We have our prophet and lawgiver in Zartusht; the Jews theirs in Hazrat-i-Moussa, and the Christians theirs in Hazrat-i-Eesá. But who is this Mohammed who sets himself up in these days as the messenger of God? How does he show his divine message?"

"The Archangel Gabriel," the hermit answered, "has revealed, and is revealing to him, the Shará, the Divine Law, which all must obey, or be given over to the power of Shaitán, and be cast into hell."

"So might I say," continued the Mobed, "that our

prophet was inspiring me with a new Zendavesta. But how will he prove the truth of what he asserts?"

He answered: "Allah gives power to those who believe to work signs and wonders. What would ye say if standing here I summon to thy presence the woman who led the tribe by whose attack this morning's victory was won?"

Apparently roused to earnest attention by this offer, Khusroo exclaimed, "Do so, O dweller in solitude, and I will say that thou art a wonderful man."

The hermit turned, and amidst a breathless silence—for all conversation and drinking had been suspended during this colloquy—pointed his iron rod towards the west, and held it so for the space of several minutes. Then in a voice of apparently frenzied inspiration, he cried, "She comes! She comes!"

Almost immediately the sound of a horse galloping was heard, and Sheereen, dismounting at the door of the banqueting-hall, walked up to the hermit in a dazed kind of state, and stood gazing upon him until after a few rapid passes of his hands before her eyes she appeared to awake and become conscious of the position she was in.

To account for this phenomenon it is necessary to state that the magnetic influence the hermit had undoubtedly acquired over her, and which has to some extent been alluded to in a previous chapter in the matter of the likeness of Khusroo placed within her view by Shápur, had been exercised by the hermit on his way to the banquet, and he had commanded her to follow him for the purpose of enabling him to make use of his power over her in propagating his new faith. She had unconsciously obeyed the command, and as he knew the distance from her camp, and had accurately calculated the time it would take her to ride to the banquet-hall, she had arrived at the exact moment that suited his well-planned design.

A whisper of utter amazement passed through the assembly as she arrived, and the general astonishment was increased when in answer to his question of "How comest thou here, Sheereen?" she replied, "Thou calledst me, and I came."

Starting from his seat, the Mobed cried, "Daughter, Ahrimán, the spirit of evil, has possessed thee. Wilt thou, too, forsake the faith of thy fathers, and follow after this pretended prophet, who has already, as we hear, commenced to spread his religion, not by convincing the consciences of men as to what is the truth, but by the violence of the sword? Can men be taught what is right by the point of the spear, and does the arrow of force pierce the brain of conviction?"

"Nay," she answered, firmly. "I see the sun, the lord of the day, that gives light and life to all created things, that raiseth the vapours and clouds which bring the rain by which the flowers bloom and the grass springs and the lofty trees spread their branches, but who is this Arab that presumes to dictate to the descendant of Noushirván what he shall believe and what he shall not believe?"

"Thou speakest the words of truth, light of my eyes,

and sweet-voiced nightingale of my soul!" said the king, in maudlin tones. He was precluded from giving vent to further endearing expressions, which might have been inconvenient on such an occasion, by the hermit's stern rejoinder to Sheereen :

"Lovest thou Maheen Bánoo?"

"More than my life," she answered.

"Go, then!" he said, "if thou wouldst close her eyes. She shall die for thy unbelief."

With a wild shriek Sheereen rushed from the hall, and in another moment Goolgoon's hoofs clattered in the still evening air, as she rode at frantic speed towards her camp.

CHAPTER XI.

A THEOLOGICAL DISCUSSION.

IT was near midnight when Sheereen, torn by a thousand anxieties, reached the camp. The clatter of Goolgoon's hoofs was greeted by the welcoming whinnying of his fellows; but the camp, although hushed in the deepest silence, presented to Sheereen's eye unusual signs of wakefulness and activity in the faint glimmer of lights moving about, especially in the immediate neighbourhood of the central tent. Leaping off her horse, which quietly walked away to his own picket, and hurrying to the tent, her worst fears were confirmed. One of the diseases common in the East, so sudden in their attack and so rapid in their course, had struck down Maheen Bánoo in the full strength of middle age, and she lay on a soft pile of skins, which formed her usual bed, only half-conscious, with the sand of life's hour-glass evidently fast running out. Surrounded by her weeping maidens, who did all in their power to restore by the application of hot cloths and fomentations the circulation in her cold extremities, her eye yet seemed to wander restlessly round as if in search of some well-loved face she had been accustomed to see, and now in her last painful hour missed. The neighing of the horses, and the clatter of Goolgoon's feet caught her ear, and her eye brightened with a flash of recognition as Sheereen, in a transport of sorrow, threw herself upon her breast, exclaiming :

"Oh, mother! my more than mother! is it thus I see thee? Look up, mother: it is Sheereen, thy own Sheereen, who has come to soothe thy pain and to weep for thee!"

Maheen Bánoo, though by this time speechless, with the little remaining strength she had drew down the beloved face towards her, and in the Eastern manner of expressing affection ran the knuckles of her hands down Sheereen's temples. Then, apparently exhausted with the effort, she let her hands fall listlessly by her side, though she still fixed her eyes, over which the films of death were rapidly gathering, on the beloved countenance. As the end was approaching, the dog, on which a fire-worshipper is supposed to look at in the last extremity, was brought and placed near the couch; but the gaze of the dying woman, after one hasty glance at it, became fixed on Sheereen till its power was quenched by eternal sleep. Sheereen had folded the poor, cold hands between her own palms, and strove by chafing and kissing to impart warmth to them, while, as well as she could through her sobs, she improvised to a plaintive, wailing air a farewell to the dead chieftainess.

"Woe to the pride of the desert and plain!
Hai, oh hai   Hai, oh hai!

For the sharp spear of death our great Mother has slain!
        Hai, oh hai! Hai, oh hai!
Woe to the glory of wood and of hill!
Though no foeman's sword, yet fate's arrows may kill.
        Hai, oh hai! Hai, oh hai!

Weeping around her, her maidens lie low;
        Hai, oh hai! Hai, oh hai!
Crushed to the earth by fate's terrible blow!
        Hai, oh hai! Hai, oh hai!
Ne'er to be folded again to the breast,
Where in weal and in woe they ever had rest!
        Hai, oh hai! Hai, oh hai!

Never again shall the horse-tail fly high;
        Hai, oh hai! Hai, oh hai!
The nomad's proud ensign of victory,
        Hai, oh hai! Hai, oh hai!
In the van of the flight no more 'twill be seen,
For she who upheld it is gone! Hai, Maheen!
        Hai, oh hai! Hai, oh hai!"

The mournful wail of "Hai! oh hai! Hai, Maheen!" borne far and wide through the still night air, soon proclaimed to the world that the great chieftainess had passed away, and that Sheereen reigned in her place. As the disposal of the dead in hot climates requires to be quickly carried out, a messenger on horseback was despatched at once to Madáin to summon priests and corpse-bearers, a particular class dedicated to this service, for the performance of the necessary funeral ceremonies before sunset. The former came out in numbers, attracted not only by the great respect in which Maheen Bánoo had been held, but by the knowledge that their fees would be paid with a liberal hand. The ceremonies at a fire-worshippers' funeral are few and simple. After the Izeshne, or funeral sermon, has been read, the procession goes to the Dokhmá, or Tower of Silence, on foot, headed by priests walking two and two, and holding a white cloth or handkerchief between them. Then follows the body, on a plain, open iron bier, carried on the shoulders of four corpse-bearers (Nusesallar): it is covered by a white cloth. Behind follow the relatives and friends, all dressed in white, and in full dress; that is to say, with large white waist-cloths folded round their middles over their ordinary clothes. As the procession moves along, the deepest silence is observed until the Tower of Silence, which is always situated on the highest eminence to be found in the neighbourhood of a town or village, is reached. The opening that gives admittance to this is near the top, and is reached by a ladder or steps, and the disposal of the corpse is effected by its being placed on an open iron grating which separates the upper from the lower part of the Tower, so that when vultures or other birds have picked the body clean the bones may fall through and remain below. The priests range themselves at each side as the bearers convey the body into the interior of the building, and there lay it reverently on the grating, take in their hands the farther end of the cloth that covers it, and walk forward with it so that they may not see the body as it lies exposed. Coming down the steps, they close the door behind them, and leave the remains to the birds and the air. Horrible as the idea may seem to Europeans, the Parsees, the successors of the original Guebres, still see with satisfaction the immediate descent of the vultures, the obscene birds of prey that soon tear the remains of their dearest on earth limb from limb, assured that the spiritual essence has already gone to that abode beyond this life where there will be peace for ever and ever.

It is customary for the friends of the family of the dead to visit the former for three days and condole with them; but Sheereen, anxious to quit as soon as possible a spot to her fraught with such painful memories, directed the immediate striking of the camp and the return of her tribe to their usual abodes among and near the hills that divide Ajam from Khuzistán.

After the sudden exit of Sheereen from the royal banqueting-hall at Madáin, the company, somewhat awestruck by what had taken place, and disposed to attribute to the hermit a degree of supernatural power, which we have seen could be traced to unusual, though not miraculous, natural causes, soon broke up, and the king retired to rest in a half-maudlin state, and to a sleep, which was disturbed by dreams of a terrific character, in which Sheereen and the Persian lawgiver Zartusht, the hermit, and the supposed new prophet Mohammed, and his queen Irene and the Christian Messiah were all mixed up in inextricable confusion. In the morning the queen summoned the hermit to her presence. She was somewhat of a theologian herself, and she desired to be confronted with an emissary accredited directly by the new prophet, just to see what he had to say for himself, and what proofs he might be able to adduce of the divine origin of his mission. The old man kissed respectfully the hand she extended to him, and commenced the conversation with the usual Mussulman formula : " Lá hául wa lá koowut illá b' Illáh." " There is no virtue nor power but in Allah ! "

"Friend," rejoined the queen, "I agree with thee, if by Allah thou dost designate the God of the Christian and the Khudá of the dwellers in Persia, the Supreme Ruler of all. There is no virtue nor power but in God. But ye, the followers of Mohammed, have an addition to this formula of your creed of, " There is but one God," that is, "and Mohammed is the prophet of God."

"Amen ! So be it ! " replied the hermit. " Such is the truth, and into the truth, thus hath it been revealed to the prophet—on whom be peace !—will Allah lead such as He will, and the rest shall be destroyed with the sword."

"But ye believe in Hazrat-i-Eesá ? " the queen continued.

" Yes," he answered ; " but not as ye Christians say, that he was born of God, for it is blasphemy, and the inspiration of Iblees, the devil, to make any one the equal of Allah, as a son would be. Allah, the Ineffable, can have no fellow ; and especially no one born of a woman ! "

" Let that alone for the present," said the queen. " The mystery of God made man is too deep for human understanding. But ye acknowledge Eesá as a prophet, and that he is Al-Maseeh, the Anointed One."

"Yea, indeed," he answered, "and on Him be peace!"

"Then did He not say that there should arise after Him many a false anointed one, or as we say in the Greek, many a Kristos, but there would be no true one?" rejoined the queen.

"But did He not say also that there should come after Him a Paraclete, a Comforter?" the old man inquired.

"He did," the queen acknowledged; "but in the spirit, and not in the flesh. And we Christians say that the spirit of the Comforter has already been poured out upon a chosen few, and that in God's own good time it will be poured out upon all flesh."

"That Comforter is Mohammed!" asserted the hermit confidently.

"Why?" asked the queen. "What proof dost thou produce?"

"Did he not fly in a single night," he answered, "from Mecca to Jerusalem? and was he not taken by Gabriel to the seventh heaven, where the word of the Koran was partly revealed to him? and doth the same angel not continue to reveal to him chapter after chapter, surá after surá, as men's minds are prepared to receive them?"

"So it may be said," replied the queen; "but the precepts of the Koran, as far as I have heard them, bear a strange likeness to the words of Eesá in the Evánjoel, and its moral maxims are but the reflection of many an ancient Eastern proverb current even here in Irán. What is beyond these breathes but of sword and blood, and our Christian faith is one of love and gentleness and mercy, falling gently as the dew. The dove cannot mate with the falcon, and there can be no agreement between us. Go, tell thy supposed prophet that we will have none of him, and that even the daughter of Irán, though she is not yet awakened to the truths of the Gospel, still believes in the one Great Author of all good, and scorns to be persuaded by an upstart Arab! Go in peace!"

"We shall see," said the old man, as he walked away with a proud air, "which faith will conquer in the end. The ways of Allah are sure; and at the last, though not for a few years, the standard of the Crescent Moon shall wave over the walls of Madáin. God is great, and Mohammed is His prophet!"

"The Crescent, indeed!" said she, as a parting shot. "One never sees it but when it is sinking beneath the western horizon, and it can never rise!"

The hermit was discerning enough to see that the time of Islám had not yet fully arrived, and that Mohammed's power would have to be much more consolidated than it was then to help to compete with the ancient empire of Irán. And thus the interview closed.

CHAPTER XII.

A STRANGE PICNIC.

SHEEREEN assumed the rule over her tribe in the full assurance of the love and willing obedience of her subjects. They felt secure of not being disturbed in the tranquil course of their lives, relying on the well-known amiability of her disposition, and on her hatred of every form of injustice and oppression. They desired to live at peace with all their neighbours, to change their pasturage grounds without interruption, from the plains in winter and spring to their cooler retreats among the mountains in summer and autumn, and to sell their wool and the coarse blankets, the produce of their rude looms, at the fairs periodically held in their neighbourhood, their numbers being recruited from time to time from among the young women of their kindred in the adjacent tribes who might be attracted to them by the freedom and happiness of their nomad mode of life, and the reputation of the mild and benignant sway of Maheen Bánoo's successor.

Shortly after her accession to her new dignity, Sheereen received, in some such little ceremony as she found consistent with the grief which time had not as yet assuaged, a formal visit from Shápur as a special ambassador from the king, sent to congratulate her on her elevation to the dignity of chieftainess of the tribe, and convey to her several horses, camels, and other valuable presents, such as the capital afforded, as becoming gifts on the occasion. Among other animals he was commissioned to offer was Khusroo's famous horse Shubdeez. This was done at a private interview he begged for after his public reception. He took advantage of the opportunity again to urge Khusroo's suit, pointing out to her that the gift of the splendid animal, which he would not part with to any one else in the world, proved the depth of his affection. Gratified as she might have been by the offer, and longing to caress the noble beast as an old friend, she thought it prudent firmly to decline both the gift and the more brilliant prospect of a share in the throne of Ajam, but assured him that her affection for Khusroo was undiminished. She could not, however, consent to his proposal in the face of the opposition of the queen and as long as the latter held him to his oath not to marry another wife, stipulated for at Constantinople when Irene's hand was bestowed upon him by the Imperial favour. Apart from the sanctity of the pledge, which the king's honour forbad him to break, she unselfishly urged upon Shápur the consideration of the tie of gratitude that bound the king to the emperor for the assistance he had given him in his hour of utmost need in recovering the throne of his fathers. Shápur, although disappointed at the ill-success of his diplomacy, could not but admire the spirit of the woman in deliberately setting herself on one side and acting solely in the interest of her lover, whom notwithstanding his imperfections she yet evidently loved with all the strength of her strong and proud nature. The ambassador, forced to content himself with her unalterable decision, returned to Madáin, and reported his want of success to his master, whose affection towards his queen was certainly not increased by the event.

Shortly after this, two events occurred, both of considerable importance to Khusroo. The former of these, the death of Behrám Choobeen, the defeated general, among the Tartars with whom he took refuge, gave an assurance of peace to the kingdom, and afforded it that rest which it so much needed after the troubled times since the latter part of the reign of Hormuz; the latter was the birth of a son to Queen Irene. The appearance of a legitimate heir to his throne was naturally a circumstance of great interest to the king, and procured for Irene a far larger share of his consideration than she would otherwise have received. The despatch of an embassy to Constantinople to announce the propitious event, and the festivities held at Madáin in its honour, took up a good deal of Khusroo's time, and the reception and entertainment of a return embassy of congratulation from the Emperor Maurice served to pass away the greater part of another year. About this time there began to arrive disturbing rumours of the failing health of the emperor, and a line of couriers was accordingly established, who conveyed intelligence from Constantinople to Madáin and *vice versâ* in about a month. They served at the same time another purpose, namely, to keep the Court of Persia well informed of the state of the country through which they passed, information which eventually was turned to good purpose by Khusroo. Meanwhile, Maurice's health not showing any signs of improvement, and he himself expressing an anxious wish to see his daughter and her child, it was determined that Queen Irene should visit her father at Constantinople, taking her son, who had been named Shiruiah, with her. Elaborate preparations were made for her journey. A special escort of Greek troops of the emperor's bodyguard was ordered to meet her at the frontier at Ctesiphon. The principal officers of the garrisons and territories *en route* were to make the necessary arrangements for the accommodation and entertainment of the royal *cortège*, and everything was done to make the journey as easy and comfortable as possible, at a time when many conveniences for travelling, except the inestimable one of well-laid-out military roads between the chief strategical points, were not in existence. Everything being satisfactorily arranged, the queen and her son left Madáin on a bright morning when spring was merging into summer, before the heat of the latter season had become so great as to interfere with the comfort of travelling. A rather circuitous route was adopted at first, with a view to avoid the bare, arid country that lay on the direct road from Madáin to Sheereen's dominion, the confines of which were reached in about a week from the time of starting.

At a particular spot just within the border, where the plain, flat and uninteresting, began to merge into the lovely wooded dells, watered by sparkling brooklets, of the hills, Irene found the place of her mounted escort quietly assumed by a troop of female riders, on hardy-looking, well-groomed mares, among which no screaming or snorting was heard, and many of which were followed by colts running behind them. Each of the riders held in her right hand a spear, the well-polished point of which cast back the rays of the morning sun, while on her back was slung a bow and a quiver of arrows. Their head-dress was the usual Persian conical cap of black wool, bound round the forehead with a coquettishly twisted white band in the shape of a turban, that to some extent served to shade the eyes. The outer upper dress, fitting the figure loosely and leaving ample room for the free use of the arms, was of a dark brown colour, derived from a dye made of the bark of a species of mimosa, and ended in a skirt reaching down to the knee. Below this the loose drawers or trousers that came down to the foot were protected from thorns by long buskins of softly tanned skins, which also served to keep the leg from being chafed by the saddle. The sole of the foot, which the end of the buskin covered, was clothed with a thick leather sandal, and held in broad, shovel-shaped stirrups, the inner side of which was sharpened so as in case of need to take the place of the modern spur. This, however, the willing and sturdy animals that bore their light mistresses with ease and seeming pride but rarely required the use of; a word or a shake of the rein always sufficed to sharpen them into immediate activity.

At the frontier Sheereen herself, for it was she who led the band, standing on foot before the queen's litter, offered on a small platter bread and salt, according to the custom of the country, in token of submission and good-will. Irene touched and tasted them by way of acceptance, whilst at a gesture from their leader's hand Sheereen's band passed half in front and half in rear of the litter. She herself, as the train moved on, took her post on horseback by the side of the litter, and rode on with it to the first halting-place, where everything had been prepared for the reception of the queen and her people. Sheds of leaves and boughs of trees had been constructed to accommodate them all, while that intended for the use of the royal lady and her child had been also thickly thatched with grass. Water from a running stream hard by had been amply stored in earthenware jars; piles of firewood for cooking purposes were heaped up near *al fresco* kitchens, consisting of two stones laid lengthways, and one across their ends, with the earth scooped out between them, sufficient for every one; sheep killed and flayed hung on the trees at a retired spot on the outskirts of the camp, ready for those who required meat for their food; while the horses and camels had been equally well provided for by stacks of green and dry grass and leaves stripped from trees. The queen's shed and those for her female attendants had been carpeted, and furnished with couches made of soft skins, and rude washing utensils of brass. All had been thought of that in such a rude state of society could be arranged for with a view to the comfort of the temporary inhabitants of the camp.

As soon as the queen had alighted Sheereen and her women disappeared to their own halting-place in a retired grove not far off, leaving a few of the latter behind them to convey messages to her in case anything more should be required. Irene had instinctively recognized in the beautiful woman that rode so gracefully by her side her rival in her husband's affections, and she was by no means surprised at the hold she had gained over him. Naturally disinclined on that account, however, to cultivate a closer acquaintanceship with her lovely hostess, she discreetly allowed the preparations that had been made for her accommodation to pass with a cold word of thanks, which Sheereen gracefully acknowledged by kissing the hand the queen held out to her as she took her departure. Next morning the march was conducted as before; but the little Shiruiah, as Sheereen held out her arms to him from her horse, joyfully accepted the invitation, and as she took him in front of her, and fondling and caressing him let him play with her horse's mane, prattled away with infantile delight until the mother's heart was fairly softened, and she fondly wished there were not between them the awkward barrier towards a closer friendship which she had conjured up for herself. As the sun grew hot, and Irene thought it was time for the child to be brought into the litter, he betrayed the first symptoms of that evil disposition which he showed only too strongly afterwards, by kicking and scratching and biting those who had to take him from his new friend's arms. The rest of the march was by no means an agreeable one to his mother and the nurse on the opposite side of the litter, in consequence of the young prince's persistent bad temper.

After the second day's rest it was arranged that an afternoon's march should be made to a camp near the Euphrates, in order that the queen might cross the river early in the morning before the day had advanced very far. The animals were to cross partly by wading and partly by swimming, and the queen and her company on rafts floated on inflated skins. As Irene alighted from her litter to embark, Sheereen again offered bread and salt, and said as she again kissed the queen's hand:

"Lady, I know full well why thou canst not look upon thy slave with the eye of kindness. But fear not; Sheereen is too proud to go where her presence would not be welcome, nor must a Persian king's oath be broken. God be thy protector!"

Irene made no reply, but as she drew her fair rival's forehead towards her and kissed it, a tear fell upon it as she murmured, "Go in peace!"

CHAPTER XIII.

THE QUEEN COMES BACK.

WHEN Queen Irene arrived at Constantinople, she found the state of her father's health very unsatisfactory, and on that account made her stay there longer than she had at first intended. Considering the not very cordial relations existing between herself and her husband, however, and her not unnatural preference for the society obtainable in the centre of the civilized world as against what was to be found in distant Persia, it cannot be said that her not unwilling acceptance of the excuse was at all to be wondered at. Here, surrounded by the choicest spirits of the age, the men most renowned in literature, in science, and in the arts, she could indulge in the tastes rendered most congenial to her by her early education, and could, moreover, associate with the most learned theologians and professors of her own religion, the free exercise of which, although perfect liberty in this respect was allowed her at Madáin, was not so easy of accomplishment as in a Christian country. She was, moreover, anxious that her son should from his earliest years imbibe a taste for the splendid ritual of the Greek Church, which might on his return to Persia make him impatient of the comparatively tame and simple services of the fire-worshippers. In this she was no doubt wise in her generation.

Being well aware of the support that Khusroo could always command from the Emperor Maurice, of whose power they had a salutary dread, the neighbouring Tartar tribes refrained from plundering expeditions into the territory of the former. Khusroo, moreover, naturally of an easy, pleasure-loving disposition, left the management of the internal affairs of his kingdom mostly in the hands of wise ministers, and thus, no cause being given for dissatisfaction among his subjects, peace reigned in the land, and he was able to enjoy himself in hunting, of which he was passionately fond. There were not wanting near him, however, restless spirits, the principal of whom was Shápur, who urged upon him the remembrance of the glories of Persia in days of old, and instigated him to emulate their deeds in recovering the territories that had passed into the hands of the Greeks, in payment for the assistance rendered him in wresting his throne out of the usurping hands of Behrám Choobeen. But profligate as he was in some respects, Khusroo had the strictest regard for his own honour, and resisted the temptation to show ingratitude to the emperor.

Shápur, over whom the hermit had latterly acquired great influence, so great as to cause the former to waver in his allegiance to his old faith and half incline him to become a convert to that of Islám, knowing

Sheereen's power over the king, endeavoured to arouse her patriotism and enlist her on his side in promoting an invasion of the Greek territory. In this, however, although aided by the power we have already seen the hermit exercised over her also, he entirely failed. The hermit found that, however, he could control her bodily actions by the mysterious power he had gained over her nervous system, when the state of trance he could throw her into had passed off her mind resumed its own mastery, and she followed the dictates of her own conscience. These would not permit her in any way to countenance a course of action which might seem to Queen Irene in the least to savour of annoyance or opposition to her wishes.

The hermit was far-seeing enough to understand that the greatest hindrance to the spread of the new faith for which he was a zealot would arise from the West and from Christianity, and strained every nerve to cause dissensions to arise between the latter and Persia, so as to weaken both, but especially the Roman Empire, in which some symptoms of decay had already appeared in the split between the Eastern and Western divisions. He foresaw that among the less-educated and more impressionable peoples of Asia the glamour of a conquering religion would seize more quickly upon the imaginations of men, and the spread of Islám would be comparatively far more rapid and lasting. He, too, was wise in his generation, and for the present, until Mohammed's temporal power was more widely established, thought it prudent not to attempt proselytism too openly. He preferred working in secret, occasionally making adroit use, when called on for proofs of the divine nature of his prophet's mission, of the extraordinary mesmeric power he possessed over the nervous systems of individuals to force them to obey him as if by the exercise of supernatural gifts. He made many efforts to gain an entrance into the inner circle of the court, so as to bring this power to bear upon Khusroo himself; but the overbearing insolence with which he had formerly acted in the first fire of his new-born zeal had never been forgotten. The king, supported by the full weight of the religious influence of the Mobeds, positively refused to see him. He therefore prudently determined to work on in secret and to bide his time.

On one excuse or another Queen Irene's return to Madáin was delayed for over two years; but the king's patience at the absence of his son and heir-apparent was at last exhausted, and he wrote peremptorily to demand that the boy should be sent home, even if his mother did not come herself. The emperor's health, too, being apparently fairly restored, Irene could no longer refuse to return, and started, with a befitting escort. Her march through Asia and the north-east of Palestine to the bank of the Euphrates need not be described. On its eastern shore she was met by her Persian escort and by Sheereen and her band.

Sheereen offered the customary bread and salt, which Irene accepted with more grace than she had previously exhibited, remembering Sheereen's parting words to her. The nomad chieftainess had now developed from a graceful, active girl into a beautiful woman, whose perfections it would have puzzled the most flattering Persian poet to describe in too glowing terms, and Irene, knowing the effect such charms would have upon the susceptible nature of her husband, gazed upon her with a half-shy, half-inquiring look. Sheereen guessed its meaning, and as she kissed her hand said in a low tone of voice, a tone that, coupled with the look of her frank, honest eyes, carried conviction to the mind of the queen: "Fear not, Khudáwund (your Majesty). Sheereen is still Sheereen, and the king's honour is safe!"

Irene with a grateful look kissed her forehead, and this time no tear fell on it.

Sheereen had brought with her a beautiful Arab pony, which she had had carefully trained for some time, as a gift for the young prince, who, being now between five and six years of age, she thought might be allowed to ride it if led by two grooms. The boy was delighted at the idea, and his mother, being assured that the animal was perfectly quiet, allowed him to put on the elaborately ornamented saddle that had been prepared for it. Sheereen rode by his side, and amused the child by telling him the Persian names of the different animals and birds they came across on the road, until his mother thought it was time for him to come into the litter out of the sun. Shiruiah then showed that his sojourn at Constantinople had not improved his disposition: he fought with the utmost of his infantile strength against being taken off the pony, and was at last brought to reason only by the threat that it should be sent away and he should not ride it again.

Nothing worthy of note occurred during the remainder of the march to Madáin. Khusroo, in his anxiety to see his son, came to meet the *cortège* on the farther border of Sheereen's country, and escorted it home. There the royal party were received with great enthusiasm. The city was illuminated, banquets on a scale of royal magnificence were held, and the poor, as well as the rich, had every reason to pray for the *ikbál* (prosperity) of the princely Sassânian house.

It was perhaps fortunate for Irene and her son that they had left Constantinople when they did. Partly from the natural weakness of his character, and partly owing to his long-continued illness, during which the reins of government had not been held with a sufficiently firm hand, and the army of the empire, wearied and demoralized by the constant inroads of the Avars, a powerful Scythian tribe, and instigated by ambitious men among themselves, who chose to attribute this state of affairs to the feeble policy of the emperor in yielding to and buying off the barbarians instead of opposing them with the full force of the Roman arms,—all these causes led to disastrous results. The chief of the mutineers was one Phocas, an intriguing centurion of low origin, and ignorant of letters, of law, and even of arms, but who had managed by the practice of the wiles of a demagogue to win the confidence of a soldiery as ignorant and brutal as himself. It is sufficient to state, without going in detail into the events that occurred very soon after the queen's departure from her father's court, that the rebellion of Phocas was successful, and he was invested by the soldiery with the Imperial purple. Maurice and his sons fled, but were pursued and caught at Chalcedon, where they were put to death by the usurper's orders with every refinement of cruelty, the emperor himself being forced to witness the cruelties practised on his sons before he was himself relieved by death. Their bodies were thrown into the sea, and their heads exposed to the public gaze at Constantinople. The queen had brought with her on her return to Madáin a train of Christian dignitaries, who, aided in their pious endeavours by Irene herself, exerted all their eloquence and powers of persuasion towards the conversion of Khusroo to the religion of the Cross. Public controversies between these dignitaries and the Mobeds were permitted to be held. By the superior argumentative powers and greater learning of the former, Khusroo apparently allowed himself to be persuaded, although he declined for the time being, at all events, to undergo the rite of baptism. At the root of his dissimulation in the matter lay a wish, seen through by Shápur alone, to excite the jealousy of Sheereen by a pretended conversion to the Christian faith through the persuasions of her rival in his affections. It was a strange situation.

The triumph of Phocas was not long-lived. As soon

as he ascended the throne he gave way to the natural licentiousness of his nature, and indulged in the exercise of brutal pleasures to such an extent as, combined with men's horror at the uncalled-for barbarity of his behaviour towards his unfortunate predecessor and his sons, to alienate from him the affections of the soldiery, on which alone his tottering rule was supported. He was accordingly soon dethroned, and suffered retributive justice by being beheaded at the same place where he had so cruelly brought about the death of Maurice and his sons. On the receipt at Madáin of the dreadful news of this atrocity, Irene, in the full belief that Khusroo was a true convert to her own faith, urged on him by the zeal for Christianity with which she hoped to inspire him, by the ties of gratitude with which he was bound to the memory of her deceased father, and by the hope of recovering for Persia the fortified places and territory ceded in return for the assistance of the Greek troops, if not of restoring the ancient glories of the kingdom, the invasion of the Roman Empire. He had become aware, through the reports of his couriers, of the weakness of many of the garrisons in the country he would have to overrun, in consequence of the withdrawal of troops for some time past to meet the incursions of the barbarians on the other side of the capital, and himself thought the opportunity one to be taken advantage of to carry out an enterprise which the death of Maurice had now laid open to him. Persia soon resounded with a cry to arms.

CHAPTER XIV.

A RIGHT ROYAL BANQUET.

IN the days of which we write, and in regions where no camp equipage was provided for the soldiery, every man on foot carrying on his own person, in addition to his arms, the sheet or blanket wrapped round with which he slept upon the bare ground, and every horseman, besides these, a bag with a small supply of grain for his beast and the necessary ropes and pegs with which to picket him out in the open, it did not take long to assemble an army. They had no thought to take for cumbrous trains of artillery for which roads had to be cleared, nor for the keeping up of supplies of ammunition for cannon and musket from a base of operations. No wheeled vehicles were in use, and the grain that was required for the food of the army and its animals was carried on camels which in most places could forage for themselves. Drill such as is seen in modern civilized armies was of course unknown. The different bodies of troops followed their several leaders and held together, and made up for their want of discipline by numbers. Supplies had to be found by the country through which an army passed, and were brought in from every quarter by foraging bands of horsemen, who swept the neighbourhood of the army's route as clean as a flight of locusts does the herbage of a tract along which it passes, leaving the unfortunate inhabitants to shift for themselves in the desert thus created.

In about two months' time an army of a hundred thousand, for the most part the mounted men of the various nomad tribes scattered throughout Persia, especially in the north on both sides of the Alburz range of mountains, had assembled on the Tigris in the neighbourhood of Ctesiphon. It may be noted here that Ctesiphon and Seleucia on the opposite bank of the river generally went by the name of Al-Madáin, the Cities; but this could not have been the town known to them as the capital of Ajam, which lies on the farther side of the range of hills to the east of Khuzistán, now known as the Bakhtyári Mountains. To attract these to the expedition no more was needed than the report that there would be plenty of plunder. Sheereen was most unwilling to join it from a fear of being too frequently brought into contact with Khusroo, which she felt would be good for neither of them, and it needed all Shápur's power of persuasion and the strongest appeal to her patriotism to induce her to join the army with a picked band of fifty of her maidens; she did so then only on the condition that she should be allowed always to choose her own camping-ground separate from that of the rest of the troops.

Owing to the distracted state of the empire in the early part of the reign of Heraclius, who had succeeded Phocas, the overrunning of Mesopotamia and Asia Minor proved a comparatively easy task. Ctesiphon, Dara, Amida, Edessa, and Cesarea, the capital of Cappadocia in Asia Minor, were successively besieged and destroyed. Antioch, Damascus, and Jerusalem were attacked and plundered; and at the last-mentioned city the sepulchre of Christ and the stately churches erected there by Helena and Constantine were either consumed or greatly injured by fire, much to the horror of Queen Irene, who, if she did not suspect her husband of being privy to it, at all events blamed him for permitting the wanton desecration of places so venerable in the minds of all Christians. Palestine and Egypt were overrun; and as many as ninety thousand Christians were reported to have been massacred by the bands of Jews and Arabs who had joined the army. The victorious army of Khusroo advanced on the south as far as Egypt and the Nile, and on the north to the Hellespont. But one little belt of water separated him from the then capital of the world.

Throughout the campaign Sheereen and her little band had followed his fortunes, and by her bravery and generalship contributed greatly towards them. Never exposing her troop to unnecessary danger in the thick of a battle, where their light arms could not have been used to any great effect, she ever hovered near, and watched it with the eye of an eagle, and wherever she saw the Persian troops hard pressed, or perceived an opportunity to assist them by a flank or rear attack, she was sure to be in the right place at the critical moment. Often had her sudden charge with the war-cry of "Sheereen! Sheereen!" turned the wavering tide of victory against the enemy, and the cheery chorus of "Ride, sisters, ride!" sung by sweet girl-voices, enlivened the wearisome march; and such was the modest dignity with which the little band conducted itself that it had won the profoundest respect from the rude soldiery with which it was associated. Any man who had dared to offer them the slightest indignity would have had but a short shrift at the hands of the latter.

Khusroo's passion for the fair nomad was, it may be imagined, greatly enhanced by her self-denial and devotion in sharing the dangers and hardships of the campaign; and it had occurred more than once that when he had himself been in a position of peril she had been there to extricate him from it, just as if she had made it her special duty to watch over his personal safety. But she was careful never to meet him except on the field of battle, or at all events in the company of other leaders when a council of war was held, so that he never could find an opportunity for again urging his suit personally.

The rule she had laid down from the first, that she was to be allowed to pitch her camp apart from that of the rest of the army, had been rigidly carried out and respectfully observed by all.

At last the Hellespont came in view; the goal of

all their endeavours was almost within striking distance! Heraclius, whom the Avars had again defeated, had sued for peace, and saw no hope of mercy in the present savage mood of the conquering Persian king, who had but lately sworn to extirpate the Christian religion from the face of the earth, after he had flayed alive one of his own generals. The latter had, after an interview with the fallen emperor at Chalcedon, ventured to plead with his royal master in favour of Heraclius, and met with this awful punishment at the hands of the tyrant, whom his victorious career had so puffed up with pride as to lead him to aspire almost to divine honours. As the price of the safety of the capital of his empire Heraclius had submitted to the most ignominious terms, and agreed to pay to Persia an enormous annual tribute, to collect the means for meeting which his impoverished subjects had to be doubly and trebly taxed, a proceeding which led to the unexpected result we will mention directly.

Meanwhile, with a view to celebrate the great event of the subjugation of the Roman Empire of the East, it was decreed that a grand banquet should be held in the camp, which was pitched within view of the Hellespont. This was preceded by a review of the army, who marched before the king in their thousands, clad in suits of gorgeous armour, or in robes of Oriental magnificence, headed by a hundred elephants adorned with costly trappings of gold and silver brocade, on which were seated the highest officers of the army and the chiefs of the nomad contingents that accompanied it. On this occasion Khusroo was seated on a golden throne in the centre of an amphitheatre of low hills adjacent to the seashore, surrounded by the Mobeds and principal officers of state in their most sumptuous apparel, and immediately behind an altar containing the sacred fire, which the high-priest constantly fed with scented wood. On the hills around stood the various divisions of the army in deep serried ranks, looking with their bronzed faces like veterans inured to war, at whose feet lay a conquered world. When about half the army had defiled past the throne, Khusroo came down from it, and, preceded by his bodyguard, a band of men in chain-armour of polished steel with the butts of their spears fashioned like golden pomegranates, and followed by the royal band of musicians playing martial Oriental airs, walked with the chief Mobed on his right hand, and his vazir, or prime minister, on his left, to a headland, the feet of which were washed by the sea. The bodyguard dividing to the right and left, the king stood on the brink, and after the manner of Xerxes, his great predecessor, cast a golden chain into the water, exclaiming in a loud voice: "Thus art thou chained with the fetters of bondage, O ocean, to the king of kings, the ruler of this world, who is obedient to none but the powers of heaven!"

Thus saying, he knelt, and looking towards the west, where the sun was just on the point of setting, touched the earth with his forehead three times. All of the vast host at his back who were on foot, as well as those who surrounded him, went through the same ceremony, while those on horseback with one accord raised their spears in salutation. These flashed back the rays of the sun, and with the kneeling myriads in front presented a spectacle as brilliant as it was extraordinary. Drinking off a large goblet of wine presented to him by a cup-bearer (sáki) on his knees, the king returned to his throne, and the remainder of the army defiled past him, the rear being brought up by Sheereen and her diminished band of maidens. She, unlike the rest of the chiefs, left her ranks, and galloping up to the foot of the throne, presented to him the butt end of her spear, which he encircled with a jewelled bracelet taken off his own arm as she saluted and gracefully galloped back to the head of her troop. "Shábásh!" ("Well done!") The shout rose spontaneously to the lips of the great multitude, who felt that the royal favour had been well earned.

Meanwhile an army of carpet-spreaders and other menials had invaded the plain, to make preparations for the coming banquet. The viands, which were distinguished by abundance rather than by anything else, were spread on pieces of leather more or less ornamented laid upon the ground, and around these were arranged carpets on which the guests sat to eat and drink, those highest in rank or in the royal favour being placed nearest the royal dastar-khw'án, the name of what took the place of a table-cloth in our more refined mode of eating. Wine cups of gold and silver were placed on each according to the number of guests it was to accommodate, and constantly filled by cup-bearers in attendance for the purpose. A special dastar-khw'án was laid for Sheereen and a few of her band in close proximity to Khusroo's own. Sheep and other animals roasted whole, and other huge joints smoked upon lordly platters of the precious metals, and were attacked by the guests with their own daggers, which served for knives, the pieces being transferred to similar plates and eaten with the fingers. A special compliment to a guest being the conveying to his plate part of the contents of one's own, Sheereen was soon embarrassed by the quantity of food heaped upon her plate by Khusroo, whom the excitement of the day had led to drink a good deal more wine than was good for him, and who was consequently pretty far advanced in his cups.

Towards the end of the feast, the chief Mobed rose, and pointing to the evening star, already plainly visible in the twilight, said to the king: "Behold, the star of thy nativity riseth to add the splendour of its light to the diadem of the king of kings, the lord of lords, the world's ruler!"

Khusroo at these words staggered to his feet, and with a sudden impulse passing to where Sheereen sat put his arm round her waist, and raising her, said:

"And this is the queen who must share that diadem with me!"

Sheereen at once put him aside with an air of gentle dignity, and with her maidens retired to her own camp.

There, after a short drunken pause, the king followed her, only to be brought up before he reached her tent by a ring of maidens who, at Sheereen's cry of, "Sisters, help me!" had surrounded her, with their spears extended in an impenetrable circle. Before the morning Sheereen and her band were on their way home to Persia.

CHAPTER XV.

A STRANGE WEDDING.

THE summit of the Persian fortunes had been reached, and from this time their descent was very rapid. Heraclius, under a show of the most abject submission and feigned despair, was crouching like the tiger before his spring. In the neighbourhood of Chalcedon, unknown to the Persians, he collected troops and assiduously drilled them, being convinced that now that Khusroo had been led to imagine the empire had been crushed beneath his feet, he would soon leave his army, and probably withdraw a large portion of it. He had the military ability to see that the success of the Persians in the campaign had been mainly due to the weakness of the Roman garrisons in Mesopotamia, a circumstance that could not have been avoided at the time owing to troops having had to be withdrawn to meet the incursions of the Avars at the other extremity of his realm. The small garrisons left, moreover, he knew had been demoralized by the insane conduct and barbarity of Phocas, which had led to that absence of proper central control, without which their discipline could not be efficiently maintained. He had no doubt in his own mind that the steady valour and discipline of his own troops would in the end prove more than a match for the numbers of irregular troops the Persian king could put into the field, and set to work accordingly to drill and thoroughly re-organize the former. In their late wars with barbarian tribes the old Roman formations and tactics had not been thoroughly studied and carried into practise in the field, and he determined to revive them. He knew, moreover, by means of his spies in the Persian camp, that the nomads were beginning to grumble at their prolonged absence from their homes, now that there was no more fighting to be done and no more plunder to be obtained.

As soon as Sheereen and her band had made their departure, Khusroo, satisfied with the terms of peace he had exacted, also made up his mind to return to Persia, and in a short time carried his resolve into effect. He took with him all the cavalry of the nomad tribes, thus reducing the army by fully a half, in addition to those required to establish strong garrisons in the fortified towns on his line of communications in Asia Minor and Mesopotamia. Having ascertained the certainty of Khusroo and the larger part of the army having left, Heraclius acted at once. Although his land forces had been defeated, his navy was still efficient, and he promptly made use of it to convey his own army to the Gulf of Scanderoon, somewhat to the south of where the Persians lay, and concealed from them by hills, so that they should not be able to ascertain his strength or the composition of his force.

Taking care not to risk the chances of a general engagement, he manœuvred so as to weary out the enemy by partial combats in many directions, and in so doing accustomed his men to the Persian mode of warfare, and proved to them that their own tactics were superior. After thus inuring his troops to war, he manœuvred so as to slip past the enemy, and, passing along by the Black Sea, he turned southwards through the mountains of Armenia, and penetrated almost without opposition into the heart of Persia before he was obliged to put his army into winter quarters, thus ending his first campaign.

It had become evident to Khusroo that he could not maintain armies at such distant points as the Nile and the Bosphorus, and foreseeing that the next struggle would take place in Mesopotamia, he recalled his troops from the more distant places for the defence of that region, abandoning his conquests in Palestine as well. This was the final blow to Queen Irene's hope of being able to exercise her influence for the benefit of Jerusalem and other holy places of the Christians. It had been long kept alive by the belief that the splendid gifts her husband had from time to time made to the shrine of Sergius, one of the local saints of Antioch, were a proof of his leaning at heart towards her own religion : they were, in fact, only the sign of a superstitious veneration Khusroo had conceived for the saint, who he fancied had appeared to him in his dreams and aided him at various times. Already embittered by her husband's too evident neglect of her, entirely separated from him in all religious thought, and having no common ties of sympathy with him except with regard to their son, her health began to fail, and this to a man of Khusroo's temperament created a further bar to their amicable intercourse with each other. As to her pious mind everything in this world should be made subservient to what she considered tended to his soul's welfare, she never ceased to inculcate on Shiruiah the vital importance of belief in the Christian doctrines; whilst, on the other hand, the Mobeds, in whose hands his father had placed the superintendence of his education, did all they could to keep him steadfast in the faith of his fathers. The natural result was that he pleased himself in the matter, and paid but little attention to religious exercises of any kind. Possessed of no natural modesty, and being submitted to in all his whims, and petted and spoiled by all about the court, he had become a most intolerable little tyrant by the time he arrived at the age of ten.

On the arrival of the news of the first defeat of the army and the incursion of Heraclius through Armenia into the north of Persia, Sheereen had conceived the idea of erecting a strong fort on the eastern edge of the Bakhtyári Hills on the edge of the desert on the road to Madáin as a kind of outwork to that city, to impede the march of an army advancing in that direction, and serve in case of necessity as a place of refuge in the troubled times she thought might be approaching when the contending creeds of

Christianity, Magianism (fire-worship), and Mohammedanism would strive for the mastery of the East. Mentioned to Shápur, who had returned with his royal master from the campaign, the project met with his warm support, and through him, with that of Khusroo himself, in the latter case induced partly by the consideration that the residence there of the object of his devoted passion would bring her within a few days' forced march of the capital, and afford him an excuse for visiting her on his frequent hunting expeditions. No time, therefore, was lost in setting to work in the matter. A skilled architect was sent by the king to superintend the building, and as stone and lime abounded in the mountains near at hand, and labour also was plentiful, the castle rose apace and was completed in about eighteen months. It received the name of Kasr-i-Sheereen, the Castle of Sheereen, who made it her chief place of residence at all seasons of the year, finding the advantage in administering her government of having one fixed spot where her subjects might be tolerably sure of finding her when they had any business to transact.

It may be as well to give here, without vouching for its historical accuracy, the tale narrated in Nizámi's poem of Khusroo and Sheereen in connection with the latter taking up her abode at Kasr-i-Sheereen, and the manner in which Khusroo's jealousy was excited by her proceedings.

Sheereen, from some cause or another, had taken to a milk diet, and found a good deal of difficulty in procuring the necessary supply for herself and her household, owing to the distance of the pasturage grounds of her flocks and herds from the castle, which was situated within the limits of the desert. On her mentioning the matter to Shápur, he informed her that he would put it into the hands of an acquaintance of his, who was skilled in engineering work of all descriptions, and would no doubt soon devise a remedy. This was Ferhád Koohkan, or Ferhád the hill-digger, celebrated in Persian romance, who incontinently fell in love with the beautiful Sheereen, and for the sake of her *beaux yeux*, set to work, and within a month dug a canal from the pasturage ground to the castle, with a reservoir at the end of it, into which the milk of her sheep flowed morning and evening without fail, and saved her attendants the labour of going to fetch it. When the work was completed and inspected by Sheereen, it appeared to her to be the work of the gods, not of a man, and she praised Ferhád accordingly. Such praise from the mouth of the beloved object added fuel to the fire of his passion, and he wandered away into the desert in a state of distraction, looking at the castle from a distance in despair, and coming at night to take his only sustenance of milk from the reservoir. The tale was told to Khusroo, who came to reason with him and endeavoured to talk him out of his madness, but to no avail. The interview is said to have ended by the king, enraged at his obstinacy, ordering him to perform the impossible task of cutting, single-handed, a road through the hill of Bee-sitoon. Ferhád at once accepted the task, on condition that if he accomplished it he was not to be forbidden to indulge his apparently hopeless passion. Thereupon he immediately bound up the loins of resolution and attacked the hill with the pickaxe of determination, and laboured at it day and night, bewailing his hard fate, and falling every morning at the feet of an image of Sheereen which he carved out of the rock. The story of his devotion reaching the ears of Sheereen, she came to see him, and out of compassion brought him a bowl of milk, which he received with all gratitude, and afterwards escorted her home, carefully leading her horse down from rock to rock. Re-animated by the interest the beloved one took in his labours, he set to work again, and went on with the proposed road through the hill more vigorously than ever, until Khusroo, afraid of the impression such self-devotion might make on the heart of Sheereen, consulted his friends as to what further steps he should take in the matter. They advised him to try the effect of the sudden announcement to Ferhád of Sheereen's death. For this purpose a hard-featured and stony-hearted man was chosen, and he bluntly and mercilessly told the unfortunate man the false story. The desired effect was produced, for Ferhád, shocked at the news, threw himself off a rock and was killed. Sheereen, much affected at this tragic event, had him buried with the ceremonies due to men of worth, erected over his remains a lofty dome, and returned in tears to her castle. Here shortly afterwards she was surprised and pleased by the receipt of a letter of condolence from Khusroo, which was the means of bringing about a *rapprochement* between them

It was not long before Queen Irene, worn out by her many troubles, died at Madáin, and Sheereen, in return for Khusroo's letter on the occasion of Ferhad's death, sent him a letter about that of his queen.

The only obstacle to the marriage of Khusroo and Sheereen was thus removed, although it seems to have been delayed for some time by his marriage to another lady of Isfahán, who had been recommended to him on account of her beauty and her other good qualities. This did not quench his ardour for an union with his old love, which—after due provision for a dowry had been made in the shape of a thousand black-eyed camels with red hair adorned with golden anklets, a thousand star-eyed black ones with paces swifter than the wind, a thousand horses with golden bits and iron hoofs, a thousand pomegranate-breasted attendants, a thousand fair-faced slaves dressed in brocade, boxes full of treasure and jewels, a golden litter, ten litters full of peacocks and sand-grouse, and many other costly gifts—was accomplished with the blessing of the Mobeds. On the night of their wedding, Khusroo, sad to relate, lay intoxicated and heavily asleep, while his bride sorrowfully watched him and sang :

> Spent with the chase my loved one lies;
> Sleep, as an infant's, seals his eyes.
> Whilst o'er his slumbers watch I keep,
> Hush, nightingale, nor break his sleep.
>   Hush! Oh, hush!

Go, nightingale, thy thousand woes
Tell in the bosom of the rose.
If thy complaint she will not hear,
Breathe not thy tuneful sorrows here.
                    Hush! Oh, hush!

Should he at morn wake unrefreshed,
Thy voice shall soothe his troubled breast;
But now restrain thy tuneful song,—
No more thy melody prolong.
                    Hush! Oh, hush!

Seek, nightingale, another grove,
And murmur there thy timid love.
Go, or thy rose for thee will pine,
And leave me here alone with mine.
                    Hush! Oh, hush!

It was not till the sun was high that Khusroo awoke, and apologized to his wife for his misbehaviour.

CHAPTER XVI.

THE SIEGE OF THE CASTLE.

THE second campaign of Heraclius had not been less unfortunate for the Persians. Having now re-organized his forces and restored their ancient discipline, he recovered Asia Minor, and steadily pushed forward into Mesopotamia, the fortified places in which one after another fell into his hands. As the Persians gradually retired, they were joined by the garrisons of the towns in Egypt and Palestine, which Khusroo directed to be withdrawn, seeing it was useless to endeavour to retain his more distant conquests when the war was being brought so much nearer home, and might, if the wheel of fortune did not turn in his favour, soon be transferred into the ancient dominions of Persia itself. In this campaign Sheereen had taken no part, partly from resentment at Khusroo's behaviour to her on the Bosphorus, and partly from being occupied with the building of her castle. The campaign ended with the recovery by the Romans of the whole of Mesopotamia, almost up to the limit of territory held by them at the time of the Emperor Maurice's death.

It was in the interval between the second and third campaign that the marriage of the king and Sheereen took place.. Khusroo would have celebrated the occasion with the utmost pomp, for he had still a large treasure derived from the plunder of Asia Minor, Egypt, and Palestine in hand, notwithstanding the expenses of the war, had not Sheereen refused to sanction it. She foresaw that the Emperor Heraclius would not rest content with the recovery of the territory formerly belonging to Rome, but would in the next campaign move forward into Persia, and patriotically desired to husband its resources to the utmost, so as to be prepared for a desperate resistance when he advanced. It required all her skill in managing her husband, and constant appeals to the real affection he had long borne towards her to rouse him to action from the state of apathy into which he had fallen. This had been brought about by the continued success of the Roman arms, against which it was apparently hopeless to strive, and the misbehaviour of his son Shiruiah. The prince, since the death of his mother towards whom he had maintained some semblance, of respect, had been surrounded by an intriguing faction at the Court, and as he grew older seemed more and more disposed to rebel against the authority of his father. She succeeded, however, in at last persuading the king to take the field in person, and determined to accompany him and do all in her power to save her country. A respectable army had been collected together, and although as queen she could not head her maidens and lead them to the fight as in former days, she deemed rightly that her own popularity would do much towards encouraging the feeble-hearted, and animating the troops with that patriotic zeal which Khusroo's late apathetic behaviour had greatly damped. She was enthusiastically supported by the Mobeds, who had hailed the death of Queen Irene as a sign of the arrest of the shadow of Christianity that seemed to be stealthily creeping over their land, and looked with great hope to the influence of their new national queen to re-establish the national faith on a firm basis. They had every confidence in her constancy in this respect, and were equally suspicious of Shiruiah, who, over-indulged and allowed by his mother to have entirely his own way, had treated their rites and religious practices with scant ceremony, or even with actual insult.

The spectacle was a grand one when the two opposing hosts stood to arms early in the morning of an autumn day to contend for the mastery in what all felt must be the decisive battle of the campaign. It was in the immediate neighbourhood of the old-world city of Nineveh, amidst whose mound-covered remains the two great empires of the West and East now confronted each other, looked down upon, it may be, by the shades of long dynasties of mighty Assyrian kings with interest, to see how the puny inhabitants of the modern world would comport themselves in the fight. Nor can the latter have been disappointed in the event, for the battle was fiercely contended and bloody.

The army of the Persians had been skilfully disposed on and about the mounds in two lines, the foremost of which was composed of elephants and cavalry, and the second of their infantry. The Romans advanced in *échelon* in alternate phalanxes, flanked by cavalry, which was not nearly so numerous as, though far better disciplined than, that of Khusroo, the latter consisting only of Tartars and horsemen of the nomad tribes. On the backs of the elephants were placed a species of towers, the lower portions of which were constructed of wood of sufficient thickness to resist the passage of arrows, so that the archers and javelin men in them were partially protected, their heads and the upper parts of their bodies only being exposed. The king and queen were seated on a magnificently caparisoned elephant on the highest of the mounds, so as to obtain as clear a view of the field as possible, and were surrounded by Sheereen's own tribe as a bodyguard.

The battle was begun by the Persian cavalry moving forward in dense masses, before which that of the Romans retired in good order, and sending flights of arrows, which darkened the air, among the ranks of the infantry as it advanced, occasionally feigning flight in order to tempt the latter to break their ranks and follow them in pursuit, and sometimes charging close up to them and casting spears among them. But to no purpose. Steadily and remorselessly the phalanxes moved on until the first line arrived within bowshot of the line of elephants, which had hitherto stood still, awaiting attack. Then there moved forward from among the Roman ranks bodies of men dragging along with ropes what were evidently engines of war of some description, but for what purpose these were intended was at first not clear. The mystery was soon solved by their being brought to a halt and beginning to throw from machines in the form of balistas blazing balls of tow dipped in oil among the elephants with a view to terrify them. They had the desired effect, for the unwieldy animals began to jostle each other in their attempts to turn their backs to the fiery missiles, and the line was thrown into confusion. Khusroo sent instant word to his cavalry to charge in upon the machines and scatter the men in charge of them. It was too late, however; the mischief was already done. With loud trumpetings the elephants turned and fled, trampling down their own infantry in their flight, and creating such a panic among them that *sauve qui peut* soon became the order of the day. The men in the towers, jolted about from side to side when the elephants began to run, were unable to use their weapons or regain control over their terrified beasts, and the whole field was soon a mass of fugitives, among whom the Roman infantry steadily advanced, slaughtering them by hundreds.

The cavalry did all in their power to interpose and put a stop to the panic, but, finding that their horses were alarmed by the trumpeting and rushing of the elephants, prudently drew to one side and awaited orders, finally dispersing in the afternoon when they saw their army defeated and no commands reached them. The royal elephant, as soon as Khusroo saw that the defeat was irretrievable, was driven off the field surrounded by Sheereen's bodyguard, and not halted until Kasr-i-Sheereen was reached late at night. The Roman general, deeming that any hasty or disorderly pursuit of the flying enemy in the face of the threatening masses of their cavalry would be dangerous, pitched camp at Nineveh. The wisdom of building Sheereen's castle was now to be manifested. It served as a rallying point for the defeated army, and was so strong in itself that it could not be taken by a *coup de main*, especially if the passes in the hills before it was reached from the West were made use of to delay the progress of an advancing army, and time was thus gained to lay in provisions, to strengthen the garrison, and otherwise prepare for a siege. These measures were now taken. The march of the invaders was impeded at every possible point. Knowing thoroughly every footpath through the hills, the native troops, which had re-assembled in considerable numbers, were able to take the foreigners at a disadvantage in many places, to cut off stragglers and convoys of provisions, and oblige the Roman general to proceed very cautiously. Time, as the winter was approaching, and the latter would soon be forced to go into winter-quarters, was of the greatest consequence to the Persians. A good fortnight elapsed before the enemy could formally sit down and form the siege of the castle, which, as it stood on the direct road to Madáin, could not be left behind for fear of affording an opportunity for cutting off the retreat of his army.

Kasr-i-Sheereen was built in the shape of a square, with a courtyard in the centre where horses and camels could be stabled, and provisions and fodder stored. At each corner was a round tower for flanking defence, and one in the middle of each of the longer sides of the parallelogram. Round the whole had been dug two deep dry moats, with a wall and breastwork between the two. Admittance was gained by a gate at one angle of the outer fortification, and thence into the interior of the *enceinte* by another at the opposite corner. The moats prevented the use of battering-rams for knocking down the gates, and the walls being of solid stone fire would be of no avail against them, whilst to guard against the latter contained in fireballs or lighted arrows the precaution was taken to cover everything inside that was inflammable with skins. A well had been dug inside the fort which afforded an ample supply of water, while outside it could only be procured at some distance from one of the small streams in the hills. Thus prepared, the king and queen awaited the siege with confidence, knowing that the winter would be on them ere long, and that the enemy dared not linger in his present position beyond the first symptoms of a fall of snow, for fear of the passes through the hills in his rear being blocked up and his retreat cut off.

Reconnoitring the place immediately on his arrival, the Roman general saw at once that his only chance of capturing it in time was by setting it on fire or by

THE SIEGE OF THE CASTLE.

escalade, for the gates or walls could not be battered down until the moats had been filled up. The former was first of all tried, and for a whole night his engines threw fire-balls into the castle: the precautions that had been taken, however, and the alertness of the garrison prevented the success of the plan. For the next few days it was evident that a great number of the besiegers had been withdrawn from before the castle, and it was ascertained by a spy let out at night for the purpose that they had been employed in cutting wood in the hills to make ladders with. All preparations were accordingly made to meet this plan of operations as well, by heaping huge stones on the ramparts to hurl down on the attacking party, and by lighting large fires for the double purpose of boiling cauldrons of pitch and of preventing the enemy from approaching them unseen.

On a dark, cloudy night about a week after the commencement of the siege the attack was delivered. In order to distract the attention of the besieged, all four faces of the castle were attacked simultaneously shortly before dawn. As the besiegers had no exact measurements of the depth of the outer moat and the height of the wall, some of the ladders proved to be too short; the rungs of some, owing to their being fastened together with small twisted shoots of trees and bushes, gave way beneath the weight of the men. The defenders poured down hot liquid pitch, arrows, darts, and stones on the heads of the assailants. Only at one point did the latter by undaunted resolution make good their footing on the outer rampart, and here they were attacked with such fury by Khusroo himself at the head of his bodyguard that, overwhelmed by numbers and unsupported by their comrades, they were forced back over the wall and few of them escaped alive. Daylight surprised the other three attacking parties while they were still struggling to plant fresh ladders, and afforded a good mark for the arrows and other missiles of the garrison, and, seeing the hopelessness of the attack, the Roman general at last withdrew his men.

CHAPTER XVII.

THE KING IN DIFFICULTIES.

GREAT were the rejoicings in Kasr-i-Sheereen when the attack was foiled, and proportionately depressed was the feeling in the camp at this unexpected check to the conquering progress of the Roman arms. It was doubly unfortunate that it should have occurred just at the end of the campaigning season, when winter was so near at hand, and there was a possibility of the passes among the hills being blocked up by snow. It was particularly disappointing, because, if it had not been for the grim impediment of the castle, which frowned down upon them in its undiminished strength, their road to Madáin lay open, and the army might then have gone into luxurious winter quarters. There had already been severe frosts at night, and a sudden snowstorm might effectually cut off their retreat. A council of war was accordingly held to consider the situation, and decide upon their future proceedings.

The hermit, in his zeal for the propagation of his new faith, had anxiously watched the course of events, in the hope that the opposing forces of Christianity and Zoroastrianism would be so weakened by the conflict that an opportunity might be afforded for the arms of the prophet to strike with success at one or the other. Owing to the steady onward career of Heraclius for several years past he had come to the conclusion that of the two the Persian power was the one that would succumb, and, believing that the Romans would not remain long in a country so distant from the seat of their own rule as Persia, looked forward to a day not far distant when the hosts of Islám might burst this barrier, and, pouring like a flood through it, create a new empire for the Crescent in the East. He had hoped that after their victory at Nineveh the Christian army would not stop short of Madáin, and was annoyed beyond measure at the successful resistance offered by Kasr-i-Sheereen. Uninvited, accordingly, he entered the camp, and appeared at the council. Finding that the general opinion of those present was in favour of retreat while the road in their rear still remained open, he urged them to march upon Madáin by the road already mentioned which led round the edge of the desert, assuring them that water and supplies were abundant along the route, and that in a week's time Madáin would be in their possession. But more prudent counsels prevailed. The military leaders, confident as they were in their power to overcome the resistance of the Persian army in the field, knew the hazard of advancing when Kasr-i-Sheereen still lay intact behind them, and the still more formidable enemy of a winter climate might any day be added to the number of their opponents. It was accordingly resolved to commence their retreat on the following day, sending detachments before them to secure the passes. The hermit, however, did not yet despair, but determined to make an effort that night through his power over Sheereen to gain an entrance into the castle. He communicated his plan only to the Roman general, who, although extremely sceptical of his so-called supernatural influence, yet promised to have a select body of men ready to take advantage of any chance that might present itself. These were stationed close to the gateway, with orders to rush forward and seize it if the gate was opened, in hope that the guard might be taken by surprise and overpowered before the garrison could come to their assistance.

By midnight all was ready, and the hermit, standing by the moat opposite the gateway, cast his spell over Sheereen and summoned her to his presence.

Straight from her couch she rose, and with a noiseless step went down the winding staircase into the courtyard and to the gate of the inner enclosure. Knowing her person, and thinking that she was on her way to visit the guards, as she was in the habit of doing, the men on duty opened the gate and let her pass out. Thence she took her way directly to the outer gate, and would have passed it, too, but it was locked. The key had been taken out and delivered into Khusroo's own hand on the previous evening! It was piteous to see the state of trembling eagerness with which she tried to force back the bolt with her hands, not heeding in the least the men who gathered round her, and naturally enough thought her mad. They sent word, however, to the king, who hurriedly arrived on the scene. The touch of his hand seemed to dispel the enchantment that had been put upon her, and in astonishment at her position she allowed him to lead her back to her own apartment. Khusroo remembered what had occurred on a previous occasion, and when she told him she dreamt the hermit had called her and she could not but obey him, felt that there was more than a dream in the matter, and fully resolved that if he once got the old man into his power the spell should be broken once and for ever.

For several hours the latter stood with the men-at-arms in anxious expectation outside the gate, and at last as day began to dawn invoked the curses of Allah on those who had frustrated his design, and went off to his solitary abode among the hills. As the invaders struck their camp and moved off a heavy storm burst over them, fortunately not accompanied by so much snow as to block up the passes, but sufficiently heavy to prove the wisdom of the decision of the council of war to retire while they were able to do so. Their retreat was not unmolested, for as soon as it was evident that the army had started back, the cavalry of the nomads swarmed and hovered round them like vultures on the look-out for carrion. Huge rocks and trees were found blocking up the narrow paths that served for roads; the water in the best watering-places as they proceeded was rendered filthy and undrinkable by mud and all kinds of dirt thrown into it; and occasionally, as they wound their way through narrow defiles, clouds of arrows shot by enemies hidden in the thickets by the side of the track picked off numbers of their men. More and more disorderly grew the array as the army pressed forward to get out into the open country. Here even they found no respite. The Persians so outnumbered them in light cavalry that they were forced to hold together closely in their ranks and not attempt to retaliate on the enemy for the constant attacks made on them from all sides. The actual loss in men was not great, for their armour protected them greatly from the arrows of the Persians; but the fatigue and watchfulness the men had to undergo were excessive, and it was with a feeling of intense relief that the Roman general after a series of skirmishes prolonged over several days saw his men safe at last within the walls of Ctesiphon and Seleucia for their winter quarters.

It was high time for the king to return to his capital. The intrigues of Shiruiah's faction had prospered greatly during Khusroo's absence, and every advantage had been taken of the continued defeats of the royal troops to fan the fire of his unpopularity which had been smouldering ever since he commenced his retrograde movement from the Bosphorus. The bow of the popular favour, which had been strung to its highest point of tension when their forward march had brought the armies of the king of kings within sight of Constantinople and apparently brought back the golden days of the Persian Empire, had flown back with proportionate force as defeat after defeat sullied their arms, and fortress after fortress and province after province were again wrested from their grasp. It needed only treachery at home, such treachery as Shiruiah's advisers knew how to bring to bear on it, to make the king's situation dangerous in a high degree. It was only the hold the Mobeds had on the general religious feelings of the people, and the alarm the priests took care to excite in their minds, that Shiruiah leant towards his mother Irene's faith, that counterbalanced the situation and prevented him from proceeding to extremities and supplanting his father. Skilful use was now made of the retreat of the enemy from before Kasr-i-Sheereen to magnify the military sagacity of the king in luring on the Romans when winter would soon prove a formidable ally to the national forces, a sagacity which the event had proved to be based on real ability. The defeat at Nineveh was demonstrated to be due, not to a want of valour on the part of the Persian soldiers, but to the accidental unruliness of the elephants when employed in a kind of warfare to which they had not been accustomed. This was to a certain extent true, and, coupled with the undoubtedly hurried retirement of the enemy from before Kasr-i-Sheereen, served to restore the good-will of the populace towards the king, and throw back his son's pretensions into the shade.

Accordingly, when the king and queen returned to

Madáin, their reception was sufficiently enthusiastic to warrant a feeling on their part that all would now go well, and that during the winter they would be able to re-organize the army, and put it in a thoroughly efficient condition to, at all events, restrict the Romans to their original territories. Political measures were also not neglected. An embassy bearing valuable presents was despatched to the Tartars on the north and east, and their Khákán persuaded of the advisability of throwing in his lot with Persia to check the further advance of the Romans, as there could be no doubt that if Persia were brought under his sway the Emperor Heraclius would not long delay to strike a blow at the independence of the Tartars also. The importance of a fortress in staying the advance of an enemy having, moreover, been demonstrated in the case of Kasr-i-Sheereen, it was determined, as far as it could be done during the winter, to fortify the passes through the hills, and thus turn to account the defences nature had provided for the country. At the same time Shiruiah's intrigues were by Sheereen's advice quietly frustrated by removing the most influential men of his party to honourable but distant posts in the provinces, so as to deprive them of all opportunity for combination; whilst he himself was made to feel that he was in disgrace by the unusual favours bestowed on his half-brother Merdaza, a son of the king by one of his numerous concubines. This rankled in the young prince's breast, with the consequence we shall see by-and-by.

We have seen that the hermit, after the failure of

his plan to betray Kasr-i-Sheereen to the Roman general, retired to his cave in the hills. Here he was visited shortly afterwards by Shápur, who conveyed to him an invitation from the king to present himself at Madáin on pretence of a religious disputation between the professors of Christianity, the Mobeds, and himself as the representative of Islám, but really with a very different object.

The Diván-i-Aam was arranged as a court of justice in the manner described in the first chapter of this history. The same officers sat and stood within its precincts, and an equally dense and curious crowd thronged the garden in front; but Khusroo sat on the seat of judgment in the place of his father Hormuz, and the culprit on his trial was no longer Prince Khusroo, but the hermit.

He stood with his arms folded across his breast, an attitude of respect in the East, and not, as with us, one of nonchalance or insolence, clothed in a long religious mendicant's robe, and with a triangular lamb's wool cap on his head, without shoes ("for the place whereon thou standest is holy ground!"), assiduously telling a rosary of brown beads which he held in his left hand. The charge on which he was arraigned was that of practising enchantment on the queen.

It had been understood that Sheereen herself would give evidence before the court, and as she was popular with all classes, the trial excited great interest. But her presence was rendered unnecessary by the course matters took. The hermit acknowledged the truth of the charge and gloried in it. There was then nothing to do but to ask the chief Mobed what was the fitting punishment for such a crime.

The Mobed prostrated himself, and then, rising and standing with folded palms, replied: "May it please the Asylum of the world! The punishment of treason against the person of a sovereign of Ajam is death, by the law of the Medes and Persians, which altereth not!"

At a sign from Khusroo, the Mirza chronicled the decree.

The hermit heard his sentence unmoved, but telling his beads walked at a sign down to the central fountain, where, kneeling as he was commanded, he cried: "There is no God but Allah, and Mohammed is His prophet! Allahu akbar."

The words were uttered, and the sword of the Ethiopian executioner rolled the venerable head in the dust.

CHAPTER XVIII.

SHEEREEN YET LIVES.

GRIEVED as she was at the severity of the sentence, Sheereen yet felt relieved that she was free of the mysterious influence the hermit had no doubt had over her, an influence to which, being uneducated and superstitious, she had also attributed the death of Maheen Bánoo. Another circumstance that had impressed on her mind a consciousness of the old man's power was the fact of the literal fulfilment of his prophecy with regard to her husband's career of conquest in the first instance and his final defeat by the Romans. It was no doubt a remarkable prophecy, but one by no means beyond the capacity of a sagacious observer who knew the character and resources of the two empires, and understood their circumstances and the relation in which they stood towards each other at the time it was uttered. She was prudent enough, however, to keep her thoughts on the subject to herself, and to let her husband feel she considered the action he had taken in the matter entirely due to his affection for her and desire to rescue her from the hermit's influence over her. Khusroo had been a little nervous as to the effect of the old man's execution, of his determination to carry out which he had not informed her beforehand, upon her sensitive nature, and her ready acquiescence in the justice of the sentence only convinced him more and more of the soundness of her judgment, and, if possible, increased his affection for her.

Everything, with the exception of Shiruiah's behaviour, thus seemed to promise tranquillity, at least for some time to come. The absence of any cause for excitement, under the influence of which alone Khusroo thoughtlessly sometimes took too much wine, had the good effect of making him moderate in his potations. He set himself steadily to work to regain his lost popularity by reforming abuses, by allowing the people to approach him freely with their complaints and petitions, by administering impartial justice in person and attending to all the details of State affairs in the manner in which alone a despotic king can hope his rule to be successful. Supported by his beloved queen with all her grace and beauty, he was in a fair way to emulate the fame of his grandfather, Noushirwán the Just, and his memory to live equally in the affections of his people.

But yet the cloud of Shiruiah's conduct on the otherwise clear horizon loomed ominously enough. He appeared bent on ingratiating himself with the lowest classes of the populace by affecting a dignity and show due only to the king himself, by promoting to places of trust in his own household men of low origin and little or no education, utterly unworthy of confidence, by riding roughshod over the prejudices of the people in matters of religion, and by endeavouring to interfere with the course of justice in cases in which his unworthy favourites were concerned. To his father and the queen he was entirely wanting in respect, and did not hesitate to intimate to his half-brothers that when he came to the throne he should certainly follow the common custom of Oriental countries and dispose of them by death or blinding. It was, in fact, only by the entreaties of Sheereen that he was constantly saved from the punishments he so richly deserved.

At last matters came to a crisis. It was the custom of the royal family on the occasion of the New Year's festival to attend at the principal fire-temple of the city, when public prayers were offered up for the safety and prosperity of the realm during the coming year, and the king received the blessing of the Chief Priest. If the king happened to be away, as in the case of his absence on a campaign or elsewhere, some member of the royal family was always present to represent him. Since the commencement of the war this duty had generally fallen to Shiruiah, but had for several years past been performed by him with more and more aversion. The new year had now come round again, and the king and queen were to proceed in state to the temple in order to show themselves to the people in the public performance of the duties of their religion on their return to the capital. It was presumed as a matter of course that the prince would accompany them, and a richly caparisoned elephant was accordingly sent to his palace, the same which Khusroo himself had occupied in his younger days, to convey Shiruiah to the king's palace to join the procession there. He flatly refused to go. Now, as this was not only an offence against the religion of the people, but a personal insult to the king, the blessing bestowed on whom by the mouth of the highest religious dignitary of the realm was believed to be essential to the well-being of the country, it was a matter that could not be overlooked; and as the prince repeated his refusal, although several high officers were sent to remonstrate with and persuade him to come, the king ordered a guard to be sent to confine him to his own palace as a prisoner for the present until he could be tried for the crime of which he was guilty. To mark his sense of his son's proceeding, also, Khusroo seated Merdaza on Shiruiah's elephant, and during the procession and the temple ceremony openly had paid to him the honours usually accorded to the heir-apparent to the throne.

The day passed over quietly. The populace accorded a cordial reception to the king and queen; but the minds of both of them were troubled with a vague sense of coming evil, which they unselfishly concealed from one another. By mutual consent, however, on that night the noise of musical instruments and the voices of singing-men and singing-women were hushed in the palace, and Khusroo, after several hours of wakefulness, was lulled into sleep by the sweet, low voice of his wife telling him stories after the manner of the East, and soothing him by gently pressing his feet. Overcome with fatigue, and her mind wearied with anxious care, Sheereen soon also fell into a sleep, troubled with terrific visions; visions, however, not more terrific than that which she was soon to behold.

The night was dark : the wind howled, and a tempest raged without the palace, raised, one might have fancied, by the demons of the air in harmony with a deed of blood. What is this form that, cowering and hiding, and every moment, as it were, stopping and holding its breath to listen and hear whether any sound stirred, draws gradually nearer to the couch where the royal pair lie side by side unconscious ? Is there no friendly dog that will raise a howl of despair to warn them of their danger? Is there no board that will creak under the stealthy tread of the approaching assassin to startle them out of their sleep? No! The floor is of smooth polished lime, covered with costly, soft carpets that echo no footstep, and the howling of the gale hides all other sounds from the watch-dog and the sentry. A soft, subdued light from a lamp in an adjoining room gives just sufficient distinctness to the noble forms lying there to enable the hand that is raised over that of the king to strike silently, but with effect. In another moment the form glides out of the chamber as noiselessly as it has entered, and Khusroo lies bleeding to death from a wound inflicted by his own son !

The Persian poet touchingly relates that, awoke by the blow and feeling that life was fast ebbing away, the king's first thought was to awaken Sheereen and ask for something to drink; but his second that she had not slept for nights, and he had better let her sleep on and gain strength to bear the awful sight that would be presented to her when she awoke. And so suffering, whilst longing for one last touch of her dear hand, he passed away while Sheereen still lay asleep and unconscious.

We draw a veil of silence over the scene that took place when the dawning day revealed to her what had occurred. Something even yet more awful to her pure mind than the assassination of her husband by his own son was to happen, which filled her with such horror as to make life itself no longer endurable. Shiruiah made overtures to her, which she, with a view to gain time and accomplish a purpose she now fully resolved upon, feigned to accept, and promised to meet him as soon as the king's funeral obsequies had been performed.

Shiruiah lost no time in assembling his partisans, and having himself proclaimed king. He took immediate possession of the royal treasury, and distributed large sums out of it both to his own followers and others who he thought were only lukewarm in his favour, whilst those he was aware were opposed to him he imprisoned without mercy. Many of these never again left their prisons alive. At the same time he ordered the funeral rites of his father to be performed with more than usual magnificence, with a view to impress the populace with an idea of his filial piety. All the nobles of the land who were within reach were directed to attend, and as many of the troops as could be collected were summoned to line the street through which the body was to pass.

To conceal his real intentions with regard to them, he seated Merdaza and several others of his half-brothers on elephants, while he himself headed the procession, after the Mobeds, on foot and in mourning garments. The bier was placed upon a golden litter preserved from former days, and only used at the funerals of kings. Behind the body walked Sheereen herself among the female attendants and slaves of the palace, bareheaded and with their long hair flowing down over their shoulders. How Sheereen managed to control her feelings and preserve outwardly a calm demeanour is shown by the Persian chronicler relating that she appeared not to be grieved at Khusroo's death, and Shiruiah had no doubt that his evil purpose would be accomplished.

When the funeral train arrived at the Tower of Silence those present formed two rows, one on each side of the body, up to which Sheereen walked with a firm step. She lifted the cloth from the face of him she had loved so long and so well, and bared the wound in his breast through which his life-blood had poured. In another instant she drew a dagger from her belt, and buried it in her own bosom. And then, as she fell upon his body and clasped it in a last fond embrace, the sweet soul of Sheereen fled to the place of the departed. In life they were one, and in death they were not severed.

Little remains to be said, in concluding this melancholy history. Shiruiah, after the manner of many Eastern potentates, either killed or confined in prison and blinded the whole of his half-brothers, for fear of their aspiring to the throne. Mercilessly he dealt with all who had opposed him during his father's lifetime, and finding that even his liberal gifts failed to reconcile the people to the rule of a parricide, endeavoured to secure his position by cruelty and the sternest repression. The one good deed recorded of him is that he, probably through personal indifference to all religion, tolerated every creed. It is not the purpose of this history to follow his career farther than to note that his reign lasted no longer than eight months.

Sheereen yet lives in the legends of Persia and the East as the model of virtue and constancy, and the loves of her and her husband form the constant theme of poets' lays.

Printed by Hazell, Watson, & Viney, Ld., London and Aylesbury.

www.ingramcontent.com/pod-product-compliance
Lightning Source LLC
Chambersburg PA
CBHW021917180426
43199CB00032B/300